BUILD YOUR OWN
SHEDS
& OUTDOOR PROJECTS
6th EDITION

Book content provided by Design America, Inc., St. Louis, MO.

Current Printing (last digit)
10 9 8 7 6 5 4 3 2 1

Printed in China

Build Your Own Sheds & Outdoor Projects Manual, Sixth Edition
ISBN-13: 978-1-58011-570-4

Library of Congress Control Number: 2021950250

CREATIVE HOMEOWNER®
creativehomeowner.com

Creative Homeowner books are distributed by

Fox Chapel Publishing
903 Square Street
Mount Joy, PA 17552
FoxChapelPublishing.com

The structures on the cover are: Top left: Plan #F55-002D-4206 on page 59; Top right: Plan #F55-002D-4520 on page 61; Bottom left: Plan #F55-002D-3000 on page 155; Bottom right: Plan #F55-066D-0022 on page 146.

Plan featured on page 1 is Plan #F55-002D-4206 on page 59.

BUILD YOUR OWN
SHEDS
& OUTDOOR PROJECTS
6th EDITION

STEP-BY-STEP INSTRUCTION TIPS

CRE▲TIVE
HOMEOWNER®

The cost of labor and materials is constantly rising. People are turning to do-it-yourself projects as a means of completing additions and renovations to their houses. If you are a homeowner, a shed significantly increases the value of your property. You will also appreciate the additional storage space that your new shed, or outbuilding will provide. This book will enable you to make a new shed, something larger than a shed, and other outdoor projects a reality if you follow the instructions carefully. Should you ever decide to sell your home, a carefully planned and constructed shed will add considerably to your home's resale value.

Build Your Own Sheds & Outdoor Projects Manual is a unique guide that concentrates on the process of building rather than designing the shed. Certainly all of the elements of design and proper plan detailing are considered, but this is foremost a book that graphically demonstrates the latest in shed construction techniques. Each step of the construction process is illustrated in detail making the construction of your shed simple and easy. Plus, several shed plans are available to order.

A Glossary of Construction Terms is provided on pages 44 and 45 to explain unfamiliar terms as you read through the instructions. Study the cutaway drawings and captions shown on pages 7 and 8 to help you to envision your shed constructed. Then, select from the wide range of pre-designed shed plans available in this book for ordering at any time.

Every effort has been made at the time of publication to ensure the accuracy of the information contained herein. However, the reader should check for his or her own assurance and must be responsible for design, selection and use of suppliers, materials and actual construction. Happy shed building!

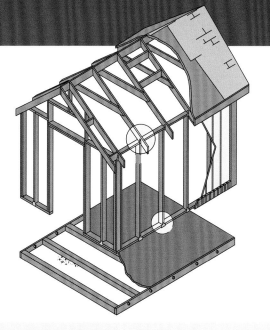

Table of Contents

Left, top to bottom:
Plan #F55-066D-0023, page 143; Plan #F55-002D-4503, page 69;
Plan #F55-002D-4506, page 59; Plan #F55-066D-0022, page 146;
Right, top to bottom:
Plan #F55-002D-4515, page 59; Plan #F55-002D-4505, page 124;
Plan #F55-102D-3000, page 157; Plan #F55-002D-4514, page 132.

3

Build Your Own Shed?

The answer is YES! By doing the planning and all or part of the work yourself, you can have the shed you might not otherwise be able to afford. By supplying the labor and buying materials yourself, construction costs can be cut significantly.

Framing out a shed is not difficult. Standardized materials and construction techniques make it relatively easy if you take time to plan and work carefully.

The key to successful shed construction is planning, planning, and more planning! Once you have begun construction of your shed, it is both costly and time-consuming to correct errors in shed placement, construction, or selection of materials. So the motto of the Do-It-Yourself shed builder must be PLAN AHEAD! Whether you choose to draw the plans for your shed following the guidelines in this manual or you decide to purchase a pre-drawn shed or outdoor project plan that is offered on pages 47-160, you must carefully plan all elements of your project.

Planning Your Shed

Here is a checklist of design information which you must gather before you begin to design your shed:

❏ **Local Building Requirements** - Visit your local building department and determine how local building codes and zoning ordinances will influence your project. Be prepared to apply for a building permit once you have completed your design.

❏ **Deed Restrictions** - Are there conditions in your property deed that restrict the type and location of your shed? Are you planning to place your shed over property controlled by an easement for right-of-way or utility access?

❏ **Climatic Factors** - Evaluate the microclimate of your intended shed location. Microclimate includes the shading effect of deciduous or evergreen trees and shrubs, the angle of the sun in relation to nearby landscaping during different seasons, soil drainage conditions, and prevailing wind and temperature conditions. Remember that an enclosed shed without temperature regulation should be protected from the sun in the summer and exposed to any sun available in the winter.

❏ **Shed Functions -** What purpose will your shed serve? Will you store gardening and lawn tools, or do you plan to use it to store household items? Do you want to supply it with electrical power? What type of storage or shelving units would you like to install in your completed shed? Will your shed include a workshop or hobby area? Careful planning regarding the functions of your shed will save you from costly changes after the project has been started.

❏ **Plan Carefully BEFORE You Begin -** All of the techniques and tips you'll need are in this book. Read it carefully before you begin construction. It will help you determine the work you can handle alone and also where expert help might be needed to do the job right. You can also learn many construction basics by studying existing sheds. Ask your neighbors if you can take a few minutes to examine their sheds before you begin planning your design.

❏ **Your Budget -** You must determine an estimated dollar amount that you want to spend on your shed. Do you plan to construct it yourself, or will you subcontract with a professional to build the shed after you have purchased materials? Perhaps you want a contractor to complete your shed project in its entirety. It is helpful if you can set upper and lower spending limits so that you can consider options in the materials that you plan for your shed. If you decide to finance your shed project, don't forget to include interest cost in the total cost amount.

❏ **Your Materials Source -** After you have completed your design work and have settled on a bill of materials, you should remember that your local lumber yard, or home improvement store is an invaluable resource for the completion of your project. Consult with your local store to check for the materials you'll need. If special ordering is necessary, determine lead times for the materials. Don't underestimate the importance of a reputable resource like your local home improvement store in providing both quality materials and design knowledge.

Planning Your Shed (continued)

The shed site plans on this page are included to exemplify how your shed can contribute valuable storage space to your home. Before you place your shed on your property, study traffic patterns in your backyard and how often you will use the building on a daily basis. Create a site plan of your property and draw arrows to illustrate the basic movements to and from your home. Establish priorities for storage locations and traffic to your proposed shed.

Be aware of problem areas that relate to shed placement. Will you need to build a ramp to move lawn mowers in and out of the building? Be certain that you have adequate clearances to move this equipment up and down the ramp. If your shed uses clerestory windows for example, to supplement or replace electrical lighting, remember that south-facing windows will provide the greatest amount of natural light.

Study the site plans shown in Figures 6A to 6D for ideas concerning shed placement. If you create a site plan of your own, remember that it is essential to locate exterior doors and windows on your plan. Try to include all exterior structures and landscaping in your plan. While a scale drawing is not essential, it is not difficult to create a site plan to scale with a ruler and pencil. Grid paper with 1/4" grids is perfect for drawing your preliminary site plan on a 1/4"=1'-0" scale.

These site plans are provided for illustration purposes only. You should sketch your own site plan first and make certain that your proposed shed addition conforms to all applicable building codes before you begin construction. A little time devoted to planning before you begin will save time and money during the construction of your project.

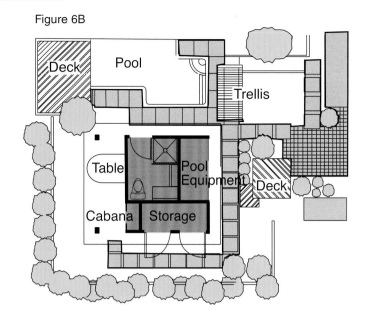
Figure 6B

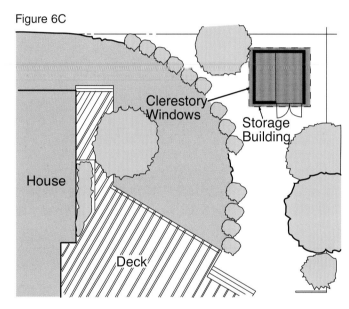
Figure 6C

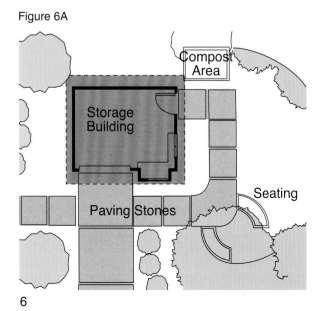
Figure 6A

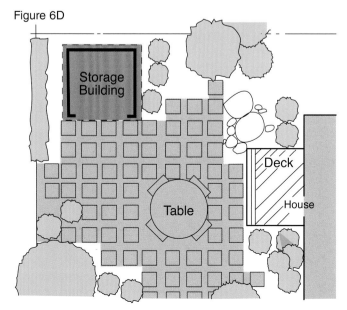
Figure 6D

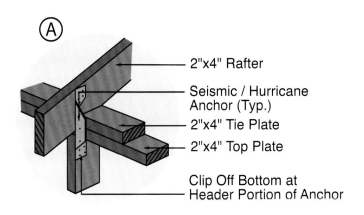

Ⓐ
- 2"x4" Rafter
- Seismic / Hurricane Anchor (Typ.)
- 2"x4" Tie Plate
- 2"x4" Top Plate
- Clip Off Bottom at Header Portion of Anchor

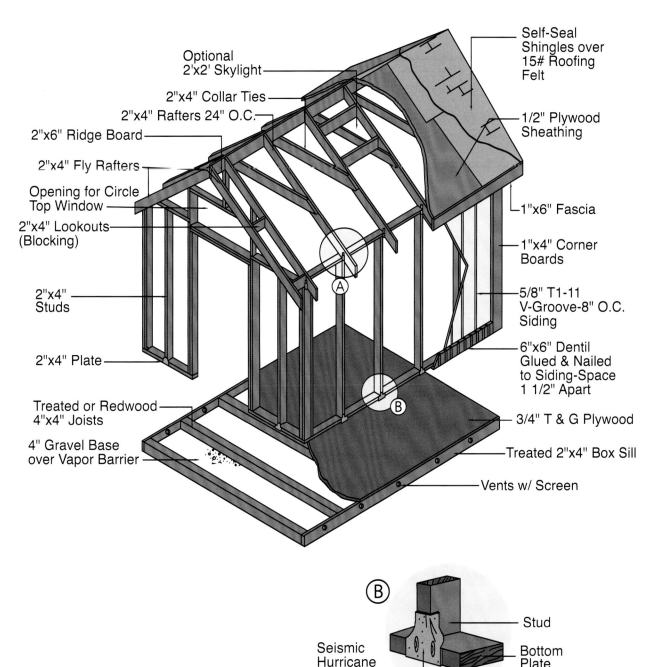

- Optional 2'x2' Skylight
- 2"x4" Collar Ties
- 2"x4" Rafters 24" O.C.
- 2"x6" Ridge Board
- 2"x4" Fly Rafters
- Opening for Circle Top Window
- 2"x4" Lookouts (Blocking)
- 2"x4" Studs
- 2"x4" Plate
- Treated or Redwood 4"x4" Joists
- 4" Gravel Base over Vapor Barrier

- Self-Seal Shingles over 15# Roofing Felt
- 1/2" Plywood Sheathing
- 1"x6" Fascia
- 1"x4" Corner Boards
- 5/8" T1-11 V-Groove-8" O.C. Siding
- 6"x6" Dentil Glued & Nailed to Siding-Space 1 1/2" Apart
- 3/4" T & G Plywood
- Treated 2"x4" Box Sill
- Vents w/ Screen

Ⓑ
- Stud
- Bottom Plate
- Seismic Hurricane Stud Anchor

Typical Gambrel Roof Shed

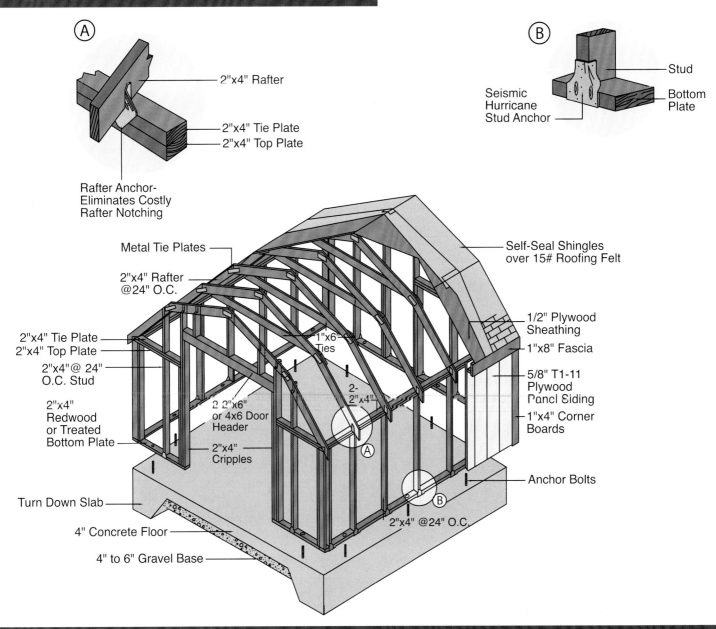

A
- 2"x4" Rafter
- 2"x4" Tie Plate
- 2"x4" Top Plate
- Rafter Anchor- Eliminates Costly Rafter Notching

B
- Stud
- Bottom Plate
- Seismic Hurricane Stud Anchor

- Metal Tie Plates
- 2"x4" Rafter @24" O.C.
- Self-Seal Shingles over 15# Roofing Felt
- 2"x4" Tie Plate
- 2"x4" Top Plate
- 2"x4"@ 24" O.C. Stud
- 2"x4" Redwood or Treated Bottom Plate
- 1"x6" Ties
- 2- 2"x4"
- 1/2" Plywood Sheathing
- 1"x8" Fascia
- 5/8" T1-11 Plywood Panel Siding
- 1"x4" Corner Boards
- 2 2"x6" or 4x6 Door Header
- 2"x4" Cripples
- Anchor Bolts
- Turn Down Slab
- 4" Concrete Floor
- 4" to 6" Gravel Base
- 2"x4" @24" O.C.

Choosing the Right Location

Before you begin, consult with your local building department and obtain information regarding the placement, height, and square footage of permitted outdoor sheds. For example, your local codes might specify that outbuildings cannot exceed a certain peak to ground height and that a shed must be offset a certain distance from property lines. If you disregard the code restrictions in your municipality, you will create problems for yourself and your neighbors. You might even be forced to remove a structure that violates local code requirements, or to pay fines. If your local code requires a permit, submit a site plan and shed construction plans to your local building department and obtain all of the necessary permits before you begin construction.

Remember that your shed will serve as an important storage addition to your home. With this goal in mind, be certain to select a location that will make shed access convenient but unobtrusive.

Sketch a traffic plan that details major access paths in your yard and around your home to help you determine the correct location for your shed.

Consider the building location in relationship to existing and future elements of your landscaping. Don't build a shed next to a tree whose growing roots will displace the shed foundation. Be certain that the placement of your shed in your backyard landscape matches the planned use of the shed. For example, if you want to use the shed in the winter, don't place the shed on the north side of a large evergreen tree which would completely block valuable winter sunlight.

If at all possible, always select a well-drained location for your shed. A spot with poor drainage or soft ground will cause problems later. Water accumulating under the shed creates condensation and can rust the materials you are storing inside.

Laying Out the Shed Site

Accurately locating the four corners of the building will in turn establish the boundaries for the foundation. The site is laid out using batterboards set back from the corners of the planned building in an L-shaped arrangement. Setting the batterboards back from the actual building site allows you to maintain an accurate reference point as you dig footings and construct the foundation (see Figure 9A).

Batterboards are made of pointed stakes connected with 4' lengths of 1x4 lumber. Each batterboard should form an accurate right angle when checked with a framing square. Batterboard tops must be level with each other all the way around. Check for levelness with a string level or a mason's line level. Consult the step-by-step instructions included below for help in establishing your site layout.

A variety of shed foundation construction methods are available depending upon your local site and your budget. If you do not want to anchor the shed permanently to one location, consider the wood skids and wood floor foundation detailed on page 10. Alternative foundation options are detailed on pages 11-12.

In areas where the ground does not freeze during the winter, pier block foundations offer an inexpensive and sturdy method of anchoring your shed foundation. Pre-cast pier blocks with nailers are readily available at many building supply retailers and provide a relatively simple foundation base for the first time builder.

A more expensive, but permanent alternative foundation is the turned-down or monolithic concrete slab. Concrete has the advantage of durability and resistance to moisture damage. If you do select a concrete slab, make sure that your slab will drain properly if moisture is released within your shed. Drainage for concrete slabs is especially important for cabana or greenhouse structures.

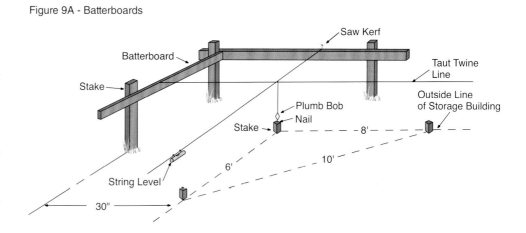

Figure 9A - Batterboards

Staking Out the Shed

1. Accurately locate one corner of the building and drive stake A at that point (see Figure 9B).

2. Measure out along the long side of the building to the next corner. Drive in stake B at this point. Drive a small nail into the stakes and connect with tightly drawn twine.

3. Measure out the approximate positions of corners C and D and drive stakes at these points. Use a framing square to form an approximate right angle at these corners. Run twine from stakes B to C, C to D, and D to A.

4. You will now erect batterboards and adjust stake locations to form a true square or rectangular layout. Erect batterboards so that each corner stake is lined up directly on the diagonal from the opposite corner as illustrated. Use the line level to check that all batterboards are level with each other.

5. Stretch mason's twine between the batterboards so it is aligned directly over stakes A and B. When perfectly aligned make a saw kerf in the batterboards to make a permanent reference point and tack down the twine taut.

Figure 9B - Layout Procedure

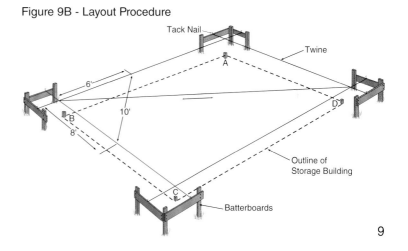

6. Stretch twine over stakes B and C. It must form a perfect right angle with twine A-B. Check for a perfect right angle using the 6-8-10 method. Measure 6'-0" out along twine A-B and 8'-0" along twine B-C. Mark these points with pins. The diagonal between these two pins should measure exactly 10'-0". Adjust the position of twine B-C until the diagonal does equal 10'-0" and then notch the batterboard at stake C and fasten off line B-C.

7. Using the 6-8-10 method lay out twine C-D and D-A. At each corner carefully measure from the point where the twine lines cross each other to set building dimensions. Drop a plumb line at this intersecting point and set stakes in exact positions.

8. Check the final layout by measuring the diagonals between foundation stakes. The diagonals must be equal in length if your layout is squared up. If they are not, recheck your measurement and make proper adjustments.

Wood Skid and Wood Floor Foundation

1. Site Preparation - Prepare the site by scraping away all grass or weed material covering the shed area. If your soil does not drain well, remove 4"- 6" of earth under the shed area and replace with 4" of pea gravel to increase drainage. Otherwise you can simply dig a drainage trench approximately 12" wide by 6" deep where the 4x6 skids are to be placed. Fill the drainage trench with gravel to ensure good drainage and to minimize the wood to soil contact.

2. Placing the Skids - Skids should be either pressure treated or redwood to prevent decay from ground contact. Position the 4x6 skids and make certain that the skids are level (see Figure 10). Tie the skids together by nailing the outer 2x8 floor joist to the front and rear rim joist. Toenail the outer joist to the skid. If you want to incline the shed floor slightly to ensure drainage, you should raise one end of both skids by an equal amount (1" for every 8' of skid) by placing additional gravel under the skid.

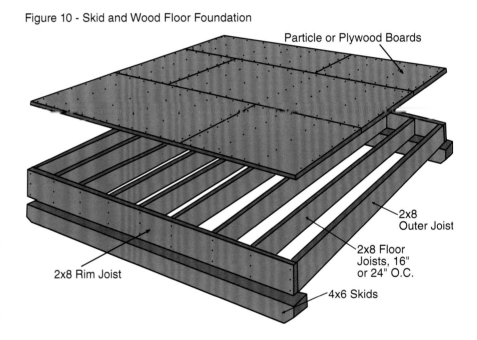

Figure 10 - Skid and Wood Floor Foundation

Particle or Plywood Boards

2x8 Outer Joist

2x8 Floor Joists, 16" or 24" O.C.

4x6 Skids

2x8 Rim Joist

3. Constructing the Floor Frame - Having nailed the rim joist to the skids, you should now check that the floor frame is square. You can use the 6-8-10 method detailed at the top of page 10 to ensure squareness. Complete the floor framing by adding the remaining 2x8 floor joists placed at 16" on center. Connect the floor joists to the rim joists with at least three 16d coated sinkers at each end. If your budget allows it, use metal joist hangers to add extra strength to your floor joist framing.

4. Adding the Flooring - For extra strength and durability, use 4'x8'x3/4" tongue and groove exterior grade plywood for flooring. For normal use, install 4'x8'x3/4" CDX plywood to construct your floor. Fasten the floor framing to the floor joists using 8d nails 6" on center at the edge of the sheets and 10" on center along the intermediate floor joists. Take care to construct a stable and even floor which will serve as the foundation for your wall sections.

Concrete Pier and Wood Floor Foundation

1. **Site Preparation** - Prepare the site by scraping away all grass or weed material covering the shed area. If your soil does not drain well, remove 4"-6" of earth and replace with 4" of pea gravel to increase drainage.

2. **Locating the Piers** - You will need to use your batterboards (see page 9) to stretch a nylon string along the imaginary outer wall line. Use this string line to stake the pier locations at 4'-0" on center (see Figure 11). The piers will support either a 4x6 beam or a built-up beam made from two 2x6s.

3. **Pre-cast Piers** - If you are using precast concrete piers with an attached wooden nailer, you need to dig a pier footing at least 14" wide and 6" deep. The depth of the footing should be at least 6" below the local frost line. Pour the concrete into the footing hole. Spray the pier with water and then embed the pier at least 3" into the fresh concrete and twist slightly to achieve a solid bond between the concrete and the pier. Make certain that you have enough concrete in the hole so that the top of the nailer block is at least 6"-8" above grade level. Check the alignment of the pier by dropping a plumb bob from the centerline string. Finally, use a level across the block and tap the pier until it is level in all directions and square.

4. **Attach the Beam Support Posts to the Piers** - Cut 4x4 beam support posts to place the floor at a height above grade determined by local codes. If you don't require posts, simply toenail the 4x6 beam into the precast pier nailer blocks with 12d coated sinkers. If you require a certain grade to floor clearance, toenail the posts into the nailer and then use a post cap connector to secure the beam to the post.

5. **Constructing the Floor Framing and Floor** - Follow the methods outlined in steps 3 and 4 to construct the floor framing and the wood floor.

Optional Poured In-Place Piers

First, be certain you have purchased enough concrete to complete pier installation. Concrete is measured in cubic yards. To calculate the concrete required for a given number of cylindrical piers, use the following formula to find the Total Volume in Cubic Yards:

$$\textbf{Volume} = \frac{3.14 \times \text{Depth of Pier (feet)} \times \text{Diameter (feet)} \times \text{Diameter (feet)} \times \text{No. Piers}}{108}$$

Note: Concrete required for twelve 10" diameter piers, 30" deep

$$\textbf{Volume in cubic yards} = \frac{3.14 \times 2.5 \times .83 \times .83 \times 12}{108} = 0.61$$

Remember to convert inches to feet (10 inches = .83 feet)
Conversion Factor: 27 Cubic Feet = 1 Cubic Yard

Mix concrete according to manufacturer's instructions in a wheelbarrow, or in a "half-bag" mixer. Use clean water for mixing and achieve the proper plastic consistency before you pour the concrete. If you are not using ready-mix concrete, prepare a 1:2:3 mix – one part concrete, two parts river sand, and three parts gravel.

Coat the inside of the forms with oil to prevent sticking and dampen the inside of the hole with water before you pour the concrete.

With your post base anchors at hand, pour the concrete into the forms and tap slightly to settle. For poured in-place piers, wait for the concrete to begin to harden and set the post base anchors into the concrete. Ensure that anchors are square and level. You can drop a plumb bob from your centerline string to be certain that your anchor is centered properly. Adjust post base anchors to the correct height.

Figure 11 - Concrete Pier and Wood Floor Foundation

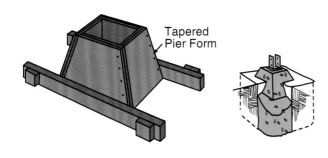

Tapered Pier Form

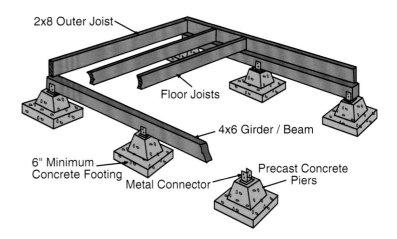

2x8 Outer Joist

Floor Joists

4x6 Girder / Beam

6" Minimum Concrete Footing

Metal Connector

Precast Concrete Piers

Concrete Slab Foundation

A concrete slab is the most permanent and durable method of constructing a foundation for your shed. However, slab construction requires greater preparation and expense than wood floor construction using skids or concrete piers.

Estimating Concrete

Slab Size	Concrete Required
8' x 12'	2.5 cubic yards
12' x 12'	3.5 cubic yards
12' x 16'	5.0 cubic yards
12' x 20'	6.0 cubic yards

1. **Site Preparation** - Prepare the site by scraping away all grass or weed material covering the shed area. Stake out the area for the slab. Be certain that all corners are square. If you are using a plan for slab construction, remember that all dimensions on the plan are to the outside of concrete. Excavate 4" of soil over shed area and replace with 4" of gravel to ensure proper drainage under slab. Level the gravel fill (see Figure 12).

2. **Digging the Footing** - Dig a trench for the slab footing approximately 8" wide at the bottom and tapering inward to approximately 16" wide at the top. The footing should extend down about 12" or at least 6" below the local frost line.

3. **Building the Forms** - Use 2" scrap lumber to build the forms for the slab. Set the top of the 2" form board to the desired floor height and level. The inside face of form boards must line up exactly with "string lines" set at proper building dimensions. Brace your forms securely since you don't want them to shift or break when concrete is poured.

4. **Preparing to Pour the Concrete** - Place a 6 mil. plastic vapor barrier over the gravel bed before you pour. Overlap the plastic sheets by at least 12" and do not puncture the plastic. If you want to insulate your slab from the earth, place 1" rigid foam insulation over the plastic provided that you have allowed for the additional height. Add two levels of 1/2" reinforcing bar (rebar) to the top and bottom of the footing and secure the rebar with tie wire held by nails in the forms. Finally place 6"x6" reinforcing wire mesh over the slab area and support the mesh with small wooden or masonry blocks so that it rests 2" above the vapor barrier.

5. **Estimating the Concrete** - The table to the top right will help you estimate the approximate amount of concrete required to create a 4" thick slab with 18" deep footings.

Figure 12 - Concrete Slab Foundation

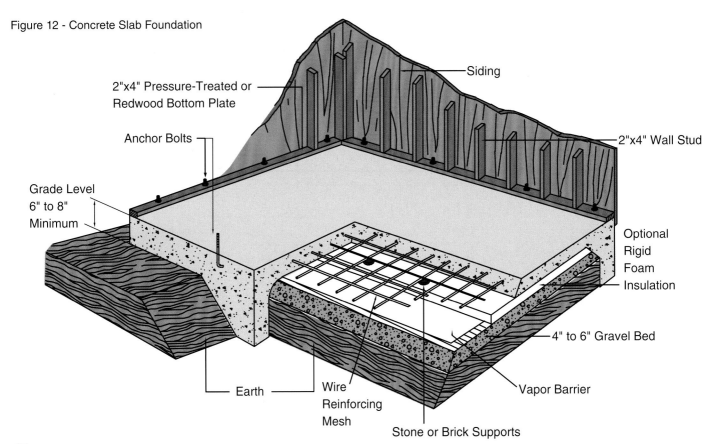

Siding

2"x4" Pressure-Treated or Redwood Bottom Plate

Anchor Bolts

2"x4" Wall Stud

Grade Level 6" to 8" Minimum

Optional Rigid Foam Insulation

4" to 6" Gravel Bed

Earth

Wire Reinforcing Mesh

Stone or Brick Supports

Vapor Barrier

Pouring the Concrete Slab

If necessary, have your local building inspector approve the forms before you pour. If your shed will utilize electrical service or plumbing, place the electrical conduit or plumbing in the proper location before you pour.

Placing

Be prepared for the arrival of the ready-mix truck or you could be charged a wait time fee (see Figure 13A). Have extra helpers, a wheelbarrow, and concrete finishing tools ready. When the truck arrives, pour the area farthest from the truck and fill the footing trench making sure the concrete does not push the forms or rebar out of alignment. For larger areas, break the work into smaller sections by installing temporary screeding guides.

When one section is poured move to the next section while the helpers screed off the first section (see Figure 13B). Ask a helper to knock the sides of the forms with a hammer in order to force air pockets out of the concrete. Be sure that all voids are filled with concrete. Pay special attention to the perimeter area of the form boards. Remove the temporary screed guides when you fill in these voids.

Finishing

Once the concrete has lost its initial shine, begin finishing it with a bull float (see Figure 13C). Larger floats have a handle like a broom. If you are using smaller hand floats, use toe and knee boards placed on the concrete so you can kneel on the concrete without leaving much of an impression. Move the float in long sweeping motions.

Anchor bolts should be placed after the concrete has been screeded and bull floated (see Figure 13D). Place the bolts 1-3/4" away from the edge of the slab. Double-check spacing of bolts and alignment.

For a coarser finish, bull floating is all that is required. For a slicker, smoother finish, use a steel trowel to go over the work once bull floating is complete. Use a light touch so you don't gouge the concrete surface. Before the concrete hardens completely, take a trowel and cut between the edge of the concrete and the form.

Curing

Once all finishing is completed, mist down the slab with water, and cover it with a layer of plastic or burlap. Keep the surface moist for four days as the concrete cures.

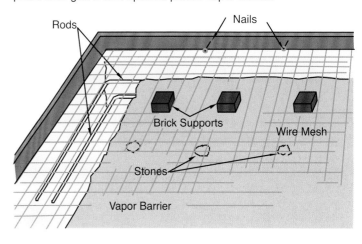

Figure 13A - Steel reinforcing rods and wire mesh are laid into place over gravel and optional plastic vapor barrier.

Figure 13B - Workers level concrete slab with a screed board.

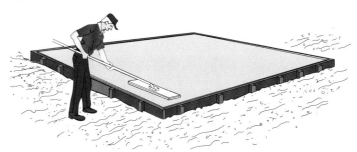

Figure 13C - Smooth concrete surface with a bull float.

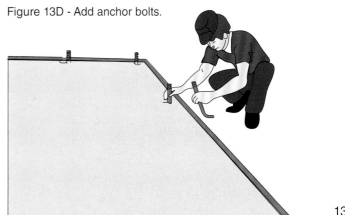

Figure 13D - Add anchor bolts.

Choosing Lumber for Your Shed

Figure 15A will give you an idea of some of the defects found in dimensional lumber. Typical defects are checks that result from separation of wood across annual rings, knots that result from a portion of a tree branch incorporated in cut lumber, and splits which are a separation of the wood due to tearing apart of wood cells. A shake is a lengthwise separation of the wood which usually occurs between the rings of annual growth. None of these defects should cause you to reject lumber outright. However, wood with a bow, cup, crook, wane, split or twist should be avoided in building construction. Dimensional lumber is typically sold in incremental lengths of 2 feet – for example, 2x6 lumber comes in lengths of 8, 10, 12, 14, 16, and 20 feet. When you plan your shed, you should try to consider standard board lengths in the overall dimensions of your shed. A 12' x 16' shed (192 sq. ft.) will be far more economical to build than a shed measuring 11' x 19' (209 sq. ft.) due to wastage.

The chart on the top of page 15 shows you how many studs to purchase for a given length of wall. You should add 2 studs for each corner and 2 extra studs for each door and window.

For example, a 2x6 board measures approximately 1-1/2" x 5-1/2" depending upon moisture content and surface. Lumber that has a rough surface will measure close to the nominal size in comparison to lumber that is surfaced on four sides (known as S4S).

The most critical factor in determining the actual sizes of dimensional lumber is the moisture content of the wood. Look for the grade stamp imprinted on lumber to determine moisture content.

Typical moisture content ratings are:

MC15 (less than 15% moisture content)
S-DRY (less than 19% moisture content)
S-GRN (more than 19% moisture content)

Standard Dimensions of Surfaced Lumber

Nominal Size	Surfaced (Actual) Size
1 x 2	3/4" x 1-1/2"
1 x 3	3/4" x 2-1/2"
1 x 4	3/4" x 3-1/2"
1 x 6	3/4" x 5-1/2"
1 x 8	3/4" x 7-1/4"
1 x 10	3/4" x 9-1/4"
1 x 12	3/4" x 11-1/4"
2 x 3	1-1/2" x 2-1/2"
2 x 4	1-1/2" x 3-1/2"
2 x 6	1-1/2" x 5-1/2"
2 x 8	1-1/2" x 7-1/4"
2 x 10	1-1/2" x 9-1/4"
2 x 12	1-1/2" x 11-1/4"
4 x 4	3-1/2" x 3-1/2"
4 x 10	3-1/2" x 9-1/4"
6 x 8	5-1/2" x 7-1/2"

A 2x6 surfaced unseasoned board (S-GRN) will actually measure 1-9/16" x 5-5/8" compared to 1-1/2" x 5-1/2" for a 2x6 rated surfaced dry (S-DRY). The chart at right shows actual versus nominal sizes of dimensional lumber which is S4S and S-DRY or better. Avoid unseasoned lumber especially in the framing of your shed. Lumber which is unseasoned can shrink considerably as it dries naturally and is certain to cause structural problems as your shed ages.

Choosing the correct lumber for your shed can be as consequential as determining the correct design. For use in a shed, the lumber you select must perform well in an exposed outdoor environment.

Performance is measured according to the following criteria:

Freedom from Shrinkage and Warping - Lumber that has dimensional stability will not cause problems later.

Decay Resistance - Generally lumber cut from the heartwood (center of the log) is more resistant to decay than lumber cut from sapwood (outside of the log). However, chemical pressure-treatment can provide decay resistance to species that lack this property.

Workability - Refers to the ease with which you can saw, nail, or shape lumber.

Nail Holding - Determines whether or not a given species possesses good nail-holding power.

Paint Holding - The ability to hold a finish. Some species which contain high levels of natural extractives (such as pitch or resins) do not hold a finish well.

Fire Resistance - All woods are combustible, but some resist fire better than others. Woods that do not contain large amounts of resin are relatively slow to ignite.

Strength and Weight - Wood that is relatively light in weight but possesses great strength is ideal.

While no single species performs ideally according to all of the criteria above, your local home improvement store, or lumber yard will be able to advise you regarding the lumber species most suited for your area. Often you must balance considerations of economy with performance. For example, redwood is considered a premium construction material, but high transportation cost outside the area of manufacture make pressure-treated pine woods a more economical alternative.

Here is a concise guide to some common softwood lumber species used in shed construction:

Cedar, Western Red - Popular for the durability and decay-resistance of its heartwood.

Cypress - Cypress resists decay, has an attractive reddish coloration, and holds paint well.

Douglas Fir, Larch - Douglas Fir has great strength and is best in the substructure of your deck, especially in the joists.

Pines - Numerous pine species have excellent workability but must be pressure-treated for use in deck construction.

Southern Pine - Southern pines possess strength but are only moderately decay and warp resistant.

Poplar - Has moderate strength, resists decay and warping.

Redwood - Premium decking material because of its durability, resistance to decay, and beautiful natural brownish-red coloration.

Remember that in certain circumstances you can use two different species of lumber to construct your shed. For example, redwood can be used for exterior trim, while Douglas Fir is used for strength in the wall and roof framing.

Whatever lumber species you select, it is important to learn the difference between the grain patterns in dimensional lumber. Flat grain lumber is cut with the grain parallel to the face of the board. Typically used for decking, flat grain boards should be used with the bark-side up in order to minimize cupping and grain separation. Vertical grain lumber, a more expensive grade used for finish work, is cut with the grain perpendicular to the face of the board.

Using Engineered Lumber

Due to recent developments in timber cutting practices and the reduced availability of certain sizes of framing lumber, engineered lumber manufactured from plywood, wood chips, and special glue resins offers an attractive alternative to dimensional lumber used for joists, beams, headers, and rafters. Unlike sawn dimensional lumber, engineered lumber is a manufactured product that will not warp and shrink over time.

Engineered lumber is manufactured to meet stringent criteria for strength, uniformity, and reliability. Glu-lam beams offer great strength over spans. Wood I-beams provide a lightweight alternative to conventional rafters. Some typical laminated veneer lumber products can be seen in Figure 15B.

Studs Required for Length of Wall

Studs Required for Walls:	Wall Length (in feet)													
	2	3	4	5	6	8	9	10	11	12	14	16	20
16" on center	2	3	4	5	6	6	7	8	9	9	12	13	16
24" on center	2	3	3	4	4	5	5	6	7	7	8	9	11

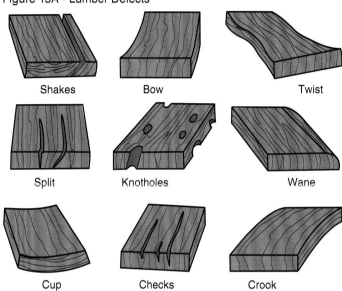

Figure 15A - Lumber Defects

Shakes · Bow · Twist

Split · Knotholes · Wane

Cup · Checks · Crook

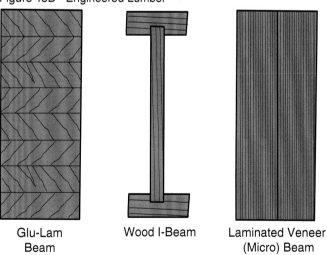

Figure 15B - Engineered Lumber

Glu-Lam Beam · Wood I-Beam · Laminated Veneer (Micro) Beam

Ordering Shed Materials

Before you shop for materials, complete the sample material list below. If you are using one of the shed plans offered in the back of this manual, many of these plans come with a complete list of materials included (see specific plan for availability). If you designed your own shed, create a material list from the final design after it has been approved by your local building department.

Always consider the quality and grade of the lumber you are purchasing. Poor quality materials will yield a meager return on your shed investment.

Don't hesitate to order at least a 5-10% overage of materials to make up for inevitable cutting mistakes or lumber defects. Be aware that dimensional lumber is sold either by the board foot, the lineal (or running) foot, or by the piece. A board foot of lumber represents the amount of lumber in a board 1" thick x 12" wide x 12" long. Use the following formula to compute board feet:

$$\text{Board Feet} = \frac{\text{Length (feet) x Width (inches) x thickness (inches)}}{12}$$

Sample Material List

	Size	Length	Quantity	X	Cost	=	Total Cost
Foundation							
Concrete							
Sand							
Gravel							
Substructure							
Girders							
Skids							
Floor Joists							
Rim Joists							
4' x 8'-3/4" CDX Plywood							
Wall Framing							
Bottom Plates							
Cripple Studs							
Wall Studs							
Top and Tie Plates							
Headers Over Doors							
Headers Over Windows							
Roofing & Siding							
Rafters							
Collar Ties							
Fly Rafters							
Ridge Board							
4' x 8'-1/2" Roof Sheathing							
Roofing Felt							
Self-Sealing Shingles							
4' x 8'-1/2" T1-11 Siding							
Windows & Doors							
Windows							
Doors							
Connectors							
Nails							
Screws							
Bottom Plate to Stud Ties							
Tie Plate to Rafter Ties							
						Grand Total	

Nails and Fasteners

Nails are the most common fastener used in shed framing and construction (see Figure 17). Nail lengths are indicated by the term penny, noted by a small letter **d**. In most cases, nails increase in diameter as they increase in length. Heavier construction framing is accomplished with common nails. The extra thick shank of the common nail has greater strength than other types. A wide thick head spreads the load and resists pull-through. For the substructure and framing of your shed where nails are hidden, consider vinyl coated sinkers or cement coated nails which bond to the wood and will not pull up as readily as uncoated nails.

Box nails are similar in shape to common nails, but they have a slimmer shank that is less likely to split wood. Finishing nails are used in work where you want to counter sink and then cover the nail head.

Roofing nails are essential for attaching roofing materials and preventing moisture penetration through the nail hole.

Screws create neat, strong joints for finished work. Heavy-duty lag screws and lag bolts are useful for heavier framing connections, such as girder-to-post.

Discuss your project with your local home improvement store sales associate to determine the best nail and fastener selections for your shed.

Table of Common Nails

Size	Length	Gauge	# per lb.
2d	1"	15	840
3d	1 1/4"	14	540
4d	1 1/2"	12 1/2	290
5d	1 3/4"	12 1/2	250
6d	2"	11 1/2	160
7d	2 1/4"	11 1/2	150
8d	2 1/2"	10 1/4	100
9d	2 3/4"	10 1/4	90
10d	3"	9	65
12d	3 1/4"	9	60
16d	3 1/2"	8	45
20d	4"	6	30
30d	4 1/2"	5	20
40d	5"	4	16
50d	5 1/2"	3	12
60d	6"	2	10

Finishing Nail Selection Chart

Size	Length	Gauge	# per lb.
2d	1"	16	1000
3d	1 1/4"	15 1/2	870
4d	1 1/2"	15	600
6d	2"	13	310
8d	2 1/2"	12 1/2	190
10d	3"	11 1/2	120

These tables show the approximate number of nails you get in a pound. You'll need more pounds of larger sizes to do a job. For outside jobs, get galvanized or cadmium-plated nails. Aluminum nails are a bit more expensive unless you are doing a smaller project.

Screw Selection Chart

Size	Length	Size	Length
0	1/4-3/8"	9	1/2-3"
1	1/4-1/2"	10	1/2-3 1/2"
2	1/4-3/4"	11	5/8-3 1/2"
3	1/4-1"	12	5/8-4"
4	1/4-1 1/2"	14	3/4-5"
5	3/8-1 1/2"	16	1-5"
6	3/8-2 1/2"	18	1 1/4-5"
7	3/8-2 1/2"	20	1 1/2-5"
8	3/8-3"	24	3-5"

The screw chart shows sizes and the lengths in which they're available. The larger sizes come in longer lengths. Most jobs call for sizes 6-12 with 1/2 to 3 inch lengths. Check size & length before you buy.

Figure 17 - Nails and Fasteners

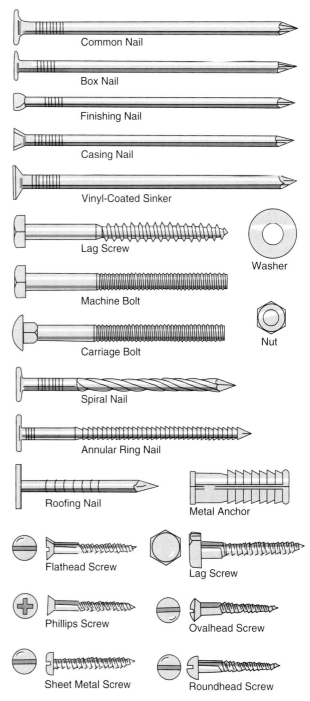

Common Nail

Box Nail

Finishing Nail

Casing Nail

Vinyl-Coated Sinker

Lag Screw

Washer

Machine Bolt

Nut

Carriage Bolt

Spiral Nail

Annular Ring Nail

Roofing Nail

Metal Anchor

Flathead Screw

Lag Screw

Phillips Screw

Ovalhead Screw

Sheet Metal Screw

Roundhead Screw

Framing with Metal Fasteners

A wide variety of metal fasteners are available to make your shed sturdy and long-lasting (see Figure 18A). You may be required by local codes to add seismic and hurricane connectors to each stud where it connects to the bottom and top plate. Rafter and tie plate connectors offer a quick method of attaching the roof rafters to the tie plate without making a bird's mouth cut. Nail-on plates can replace plywood gussets in gambrel roof construction and help create a rigid roof frame. Always follow the manufacturer's installation instructions.

Right-angled corner framing anchors add strength to perpendicular butt joints, especially where rim joists meet. Use joist hangers to attach your floor joists to rim joist members. Beam connectors provide a strong connection between beams and posts or pier blocks. The modest additional expense of metal fasteners will be more than offset by the added durability of your shed. Secure fasteners using the short ribbed nails provided or where extra strength is required use lag screws in addition to nails.

Figure 18A - Variety of Metal Fasteners

Joist Hanger

Girder/Beam Base Connector

Rafter Anchor

Nail-On Plate Connector

Seismic/Hurricane Rafter Anchor

Corner Framing Anchor

Seismic/Hurricane Stud Plate Anchor

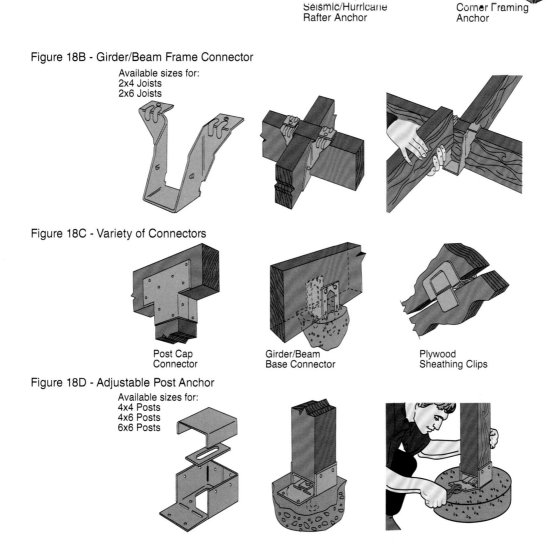

Figure 18B - Girder/Beam Frame Connector

Available sizes for:
2x4 Joists
2x6 Joists

Figure 18C - Variety of Connectors

Post Cap Connector

Girder/Beam Base Connector

Plywood Sheathing Clips

Figure 18D - Adjustable Post Anchor

Available sizes for:
4x4 Posts
4x6 Posts
6x6 Posts

Typical Shed Floor Plan

Floor Framing Plan

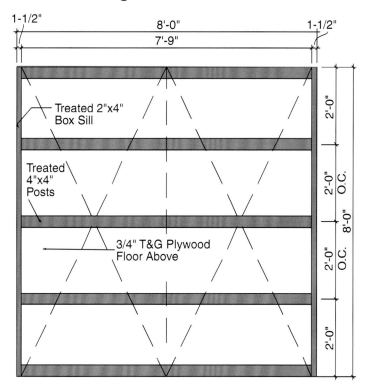

1-1/2"   8'-0"   1-1/2"
7'-9"

Treated 2"x4"
Box Sill

Treated
4"x4"
Posts

3/4" T&G Plywood
Floor Above

2'-0"
2'-0" O.C.
2'-0" O.C.
2'-0"
8'-0"

Floor Plan

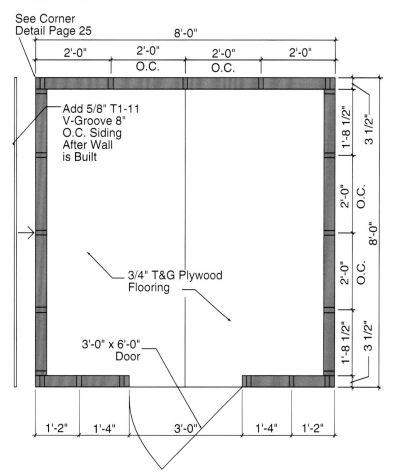

See Corner
Detail Page 25

8'-0"

2'-0"   2'-0"   2'-0"   2'-0"
O.C.   O.C.

Add 5/8" T1-11
V-Groove 8"
O.C. Siding
After Wall
is Built

3/4" T&G Plywood
Flooring

3'-0" x 6'-0"
Door

1'-8 1/2"   3 1/2"
2'-0" O.C.
8'-0"
2'-0" O.C.
1'-8 1/2"   3 1/2"

1'-2"   1'-4"   3'-0"   1'-4"   1'-2"

Rear Wall Framing Plan

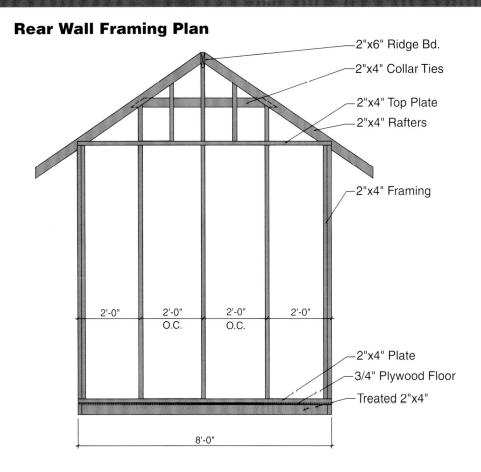

2"x6" Ridge Bd.

2"x4" Collar Ties

2"x4" Top Plate

2"x4" Rafters

2"x4" Framing

2'-0" 2'-0" O.C. 2'-0" O.C. 2'-0"

2"x4" Plate

3/4" Plywood Floor

Treated 2"x4"

8'-0"

Side Wall Framing Plan

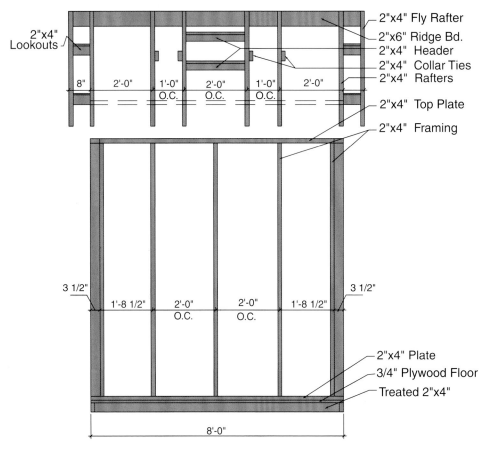

2"x4" Lookouts

2"x4" Fly Rafter

2"x6" Ridge Bd.

2"x4" Header

2"x4" Collar Ties

2"x4" Rafters

2"x4" Top Plate

2"x4" Framing

8" 2'-0" 1'-0" O.C. 2'-0" O.C. 1'-0" O.C. 2'-0"

3 1/2" 1'-8 1/2" 2'-0" O.C. 2'-0" O.C. 1'-8 1/2" 3 1/2"

2"x4" Plate

3/4" Plywood Floor

Treated 2"x4"

8'-0"

Constructing the Basic Wall Frame

To begin, cut both the top and bottom plates to length. In most cases, you will need more than one piece of lumber for each plate. Locate the joints at stud centers and offset joints between top and bottom plates by at least 4'-0" (see Figure 21).

Lay the top plate against the bottom plate on the floor as illustrated below. Beginning at one end, measure 15-1/4" in and draw a line across both plates. Measure out farther along the plates an additional distance of 1-1/2" from this line, and draw a second line. The first interior stud will be placed between these lines. From these lines, advance 16" at a time, drawing new lines, until you reach the far end of the plates. Each set of lines will outline the placement of a stud with all studs evenly spaced at 16" on center. If you are using studs on 24" centers, the first measurement in from the edge would be 23-1/4".

Figure 21 - Assembling the Wall Frame

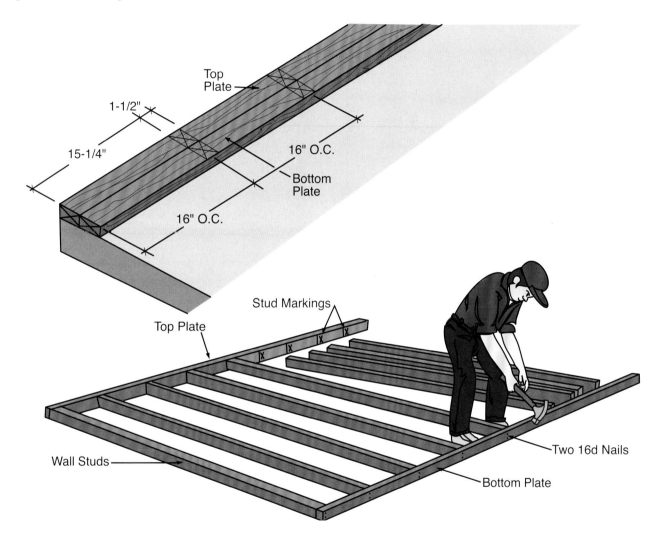

Assembling the Pieces

If you are using precut studs (either 92-1/4" or 92-5/8" in length), no cutting is required. Otherwise, measure and cut the wall studs to exact length. Position the plates apart on the floor and turn them on edge with the stud marking toward the center. Place the studs between the lines and nail them through each plate with two 16d common nails.

Framing Corners

Where walls meet, you might need extra studs to handle the corner tie to the adjacent wall. These extra studs should be added to the ends of the longer two of the four walls. The exact positioning of these extra corner studs is shown on page 25.

Door and Window Framing

At door and window openings there is no stud support, so a header is required. Door and window headers can be constructed either from 4x dimensional lumber, veneer laminate lumber also known as engineered lumber, or two lengths of 2x material on edge with a 1/2" piece of plywood sandwiched between them (see Figure 22A). When you are constructing a built-up header from doubled-up 2x material, the plywood makes the header the same 3-1/2" width as the studs.

Headers are always installed on edge as shown. Consult the chart below to determine the header size required for a given span.

The spaces above door openings and above and below windows are framed with cripple studs spaced 16" on center (see Figure 22B). Study the illustrations to become familiar with the king and trimmer stud locations used in framing doors and windows.

The rough framed door should be 1-1/2" higher than the usual 80" actual door height and 2-1/2" wider than the door to account for doorjamb material. When the 1-1/2" bottom plate is cut from the opening, this adds the needed 1-1/2" in extra height.

In addition to cripple studs, king studs, and trimmer studs, window framing also uses a rough sill to support the window. Window headers should be set at the same time as door headers. Consult the manufacturer's instructions for a suggested rough-out opening to accommodate a given window.

Header Assembly

Nail two pieces of 2xs and plywood to the length between king studs with 16d nails spaced 16" apart along both top and bottom edges.

Figure 22A - Header Assembly

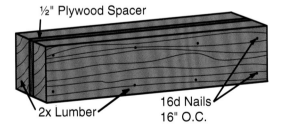

½" Plywood Spacer

2x Lumber

16d Nails
16" O.C.

Header Size (4x or built-up 2x)	Maximum Span (feet)
4 x 4	4'
4 x 6	6'
4 x 8	8'
4 x 10	10'
4 x 12	12'

Figure 22B - Door and Window Framing

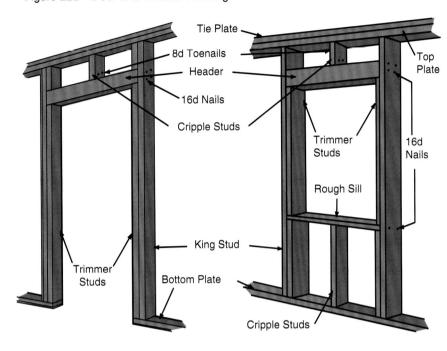

Tie Plate

8d Toenails

Header

16d Nails

Cripple Studs

Top Plate

Trimmer Studs

16d Nails

Rough Sill

King Stud

Trimmer Studs

Bottom Plate

Cripple Studs

Figure 22C - Wall Framing

Tie Plate

Top Plate

Wall Studs

Diagonal Corner Bracing

Bottom Plate

Diagonal Bracing

Structures with plywood siding do not normally require bracing, but all others do. The two most commonly used types of bracing are wooden "let-in" bracing made of 1x4 stock and metal step bracing.

Let-in Bracing

This type of wooden bracing runs from the top outside corners of the wall to the bottom center of the wall (see Figure 23A). It forms a V-shaped configuration as shown on page 22. These braces are set into notched studs and are prepared while the wall frame is still lying on the slab.

Lay the 1x4 on the frame with one end at a top corner and the other end as far out on the bottom plate as possible without running into any door or window opening. Mark the underside of the brace where it overhangs the top and bottom plates to determine the angle at which the plates cross. Also mark both studs and plates at each point the brace crosses them. Notch the studs at these locations by making repeated cuts with your circular saw. Use a hammer and wood chisel to knock out any stubborn chips. Trim the ends of the 1x4 and put the brace in place. Hold it in place with a single nail until the wall is raised and plumbed. Then nail the brace fast with 8d nails wherever it crosses a plate or stud.

Metal Strap Bracing

Commonly available in 10' to 12' lengths, this type of bracing is nailed to the outside of the studded walls after they are raised, square, and plumb (see Figure 23B). Metal bracing is thin enough not to obstruct the exterior wall sheathing.

The straps have predrilled holes every 2" sized to accept an 8d nail. Strap bracing must always be installed in crossed pairs, similar to a large X design.

Figure 23B -
Alternative Metal Strap

Figure 23A - Bracing

Step 1
Mark bracing locations.

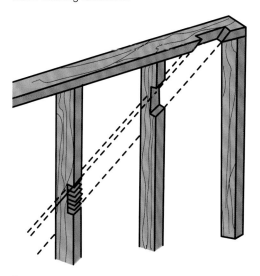

Step 2
Notch out studs.

Step 3
Nail bracing into stud locations.

23

Raising the Walls

Most walls can be raised by hand if enough help is available on the job site. It is advisable to have one person for every 10' of wall for the lifting operation.

The order in which walls are framed and raised can vary from job to job, but in general, the longer exterior walls are framed first. The shorter exterior walls are then raised and the corners are nailed together.

Once the first wall is framed out, there are only a few short steps until it is up and standing. If you are raising a wall on a slab, slide the wall along the slab until the bottom plate lies near the anchor bolt at the floor's edge. If you are raising a wall on a wood floor, you might want to tack some scrap lumber along the floor rim joists to prevent the wall from slipping over the edge. To raise the wall, you should have your workers grip it at the top plate in unison and work their hands beneath the plate (see Figure 24). Now everyone walks down the wall until it is in the upright position. On a slab you need to slip the bottom plate in place over the anchor bolts as you tilt the wall up.

To brace the wall, tack 2x4 braces to the wall studs, one at each end, and one in the middle if the wall is particularly long. Tie these braces into stakes driven firmly into the ground, or tack them to the wood floor rim joists if appropriate. Secure the wall by using washers and nuts if you have anchor bolts, or tack the bottom plate to the wood floor. Do not securely nail the bottom plate to the floor until you are certain that the wall is in proper alignment.

To check alignment, use a carpenter's level to check the wall for plumb along both end studs on adjacent faces. If the wall is out of plumb, loosen that brace, align the wall, and secure the brace again. If an end stud is warped, bridge the warp with a straight board. When both ends are plumb, adjust the middle.

Figure 24 - To raise the wall, have your workers grip it at the top plate in unison and work their hands beneath the plate. Now everyone walks until it is in the upright position. To check alignment, use a carpenter's level.

Leveling and Corner Details

Once raised, the wall should also be checked for levelness. If needed, it can be shimmed level using tapered cedar shingles driven between the foundation and the bottom plate. Once the wall is plumb and level, tighten the anchor nuts to their final tightness or on wooden floors nail two 16d common nails between each stud. Do not nail the bottom plate in a door opening since this section must be cut out for the door.

At corners, nail through the end walls into the stud using 16d common nails staggered every 12". When the walls are up, you can then add the 2x4 tie plates to the top plates on each wall. These tie plates lap over onto adjacent walls to interlock the walls and give added strength to the structure.

Figure 25A - Corner Detail From Above

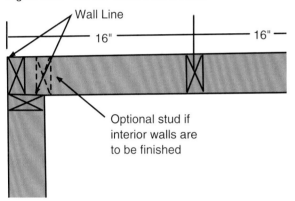

Figure 25B - Leveling Wall

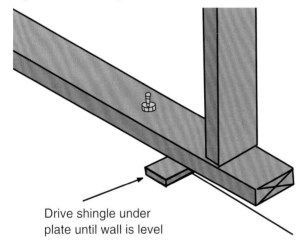

Figure 25C - Corner Detail From Side

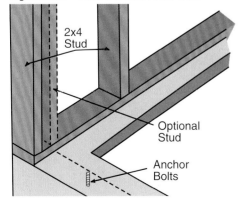

Nailing Schedule for Structural Members

Description of Building Materials	Number & Type of Fastener	Spacing of Fasteners
Top or sole plate to stud, end nail	2-16d	-
Stud to sole plate, toenail	4-8d or 3-16d	-
Doubled studs, face nail	16d	24" O.C.
Doubled top plates, face nail	16d	16" O.C.
Top plates, taps and intersections, face nail	2-16d	-
Header, two pieces	16d	16" O.C. along each edge
Ceiling joists to plate, toenail	2-16d	-
Continuous header to stud, toenail	4-8d	-
Ceiling joist, taps over partitions, face nail	3-16d	-
Ceiling joist to parallel rafters, face nail	3-16d	-
Rafter to plate, toenail	2-16d	-
1" brace to each stud and plate, face nail	2-8d	-
Built-up corner studs	16d	30" O.C.
Built-up girder and beams	16d	32" O.C. at top & bottom & staggered 2-20d at ends & at each splice
Roof rafters to ridge, valley or hip rafters, toe nail	4-16d	-
Face nail	3-16d	-
Collar ties to rafters, face nail	3-8d	-

Description of Building Materials	Description of Fasteners	Spacing of Fasteners
Roof and wall sheathing to frame		
1/2 inch to 5/16 inch roof & wall sheathing to frame	6d	6" O.C. edges 12" O.C. at intermediate supports
Other wall sheathing		
1/2 inch fiberboard sheathing	1 1/2" galvanized roofing nail 6d common nail	3" O.C. at edges 6" O.C. at intermediate supports

Figure 25D - Corner Detail Top Plates

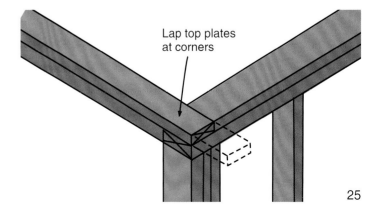

Roof Framing

Most roof designs are variations of the gable roof, in which evenly spaced pairs of common rafters join the tie plates and central ridge board together. A hip roof is also used in shed construction and most often utilizes small hip roof trusses to create the roof framing. Rafters are 2x4s, 2x6s, or 2x8s depending upon span, spacing, load, and roof slope. They are installed on 16" or 24" centers. Check with your local building department for help regarding rafter requirements and roof load in your area. At the peak, rafter boards butt against a central ridge board. The ridge board can be either 1x or 2x lumber and is one size wider than the rafter lumber. Slope, or pitch, is referred to in terms of unit rise in a given unit run. Unit run is fixed at 12 inches. Unit rise is the slope over those 12 inches. A rise of 4" over 12" equals a slope of 4 in 12".

Cutting the Rafters

A common rafter has three cuts: the plumb cut to form the angle where the rafter meets the ridge board, the bird's mouth notch to fit the top plate, and the tail cut at the end of the overhang. Professionally designed plans, like those available in this book, often have a template or diagram that serves as a master for rafter cutting. Cut two rafters off of the master and check them for accuracy before cutting the others. Use a steel carpenter's square to mark the cuts.

Raising the Roof

With the ridge board and rafters cut, you can raise the roof. Unless the roof is small, you'll need a minimum of three people. Nail an upright 2x4 for each of the end rafters flush against the middle of the end top plate. One person then lines up one end of the rafter with the end of the side top plate and ties it in with three 16d nails. The second raises and holds it at the correct slope against one of the 2x4s, while the third person tacks the two together. Do the same with the opposite end rafter, then align the ridge board between the top of the rafters and tie it in with three 16d common nails through each rafter. Use 8d common nails if the ridge board is 1x common lumber. The ridge board must be level, and the rafter ends must be flush with the sides of the ridge board. Repeat the process at the opposite end for a single-piece ridge board. For a two-piece ridge board, connect the rafters to the last spacing mark at the opposite end.

Figure 26 - For those of us not familiar with a square, lay out the initial pair of rafters on the slab. Snap chalk lines to represent the bottom of the rafters and the plate line. Use the rise in 12" to establish the angle (for example, 4" in 12"). If they fit, use them as patterns for all other rafters.

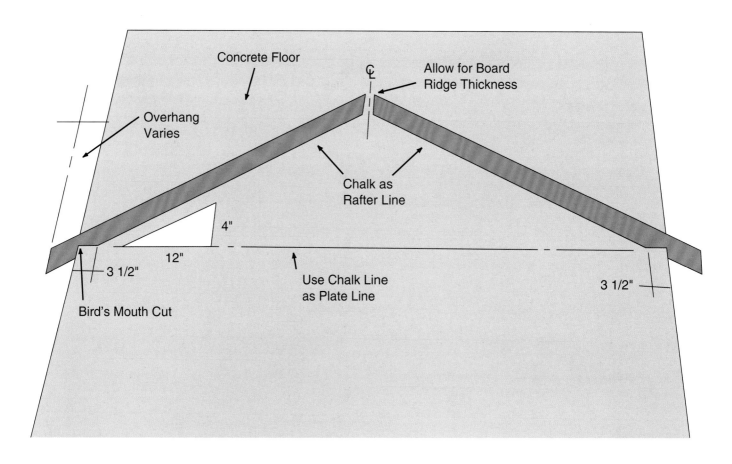

Roof Framing (continued)

Figure 27A - Typical Storage Building Section
(for reference only)

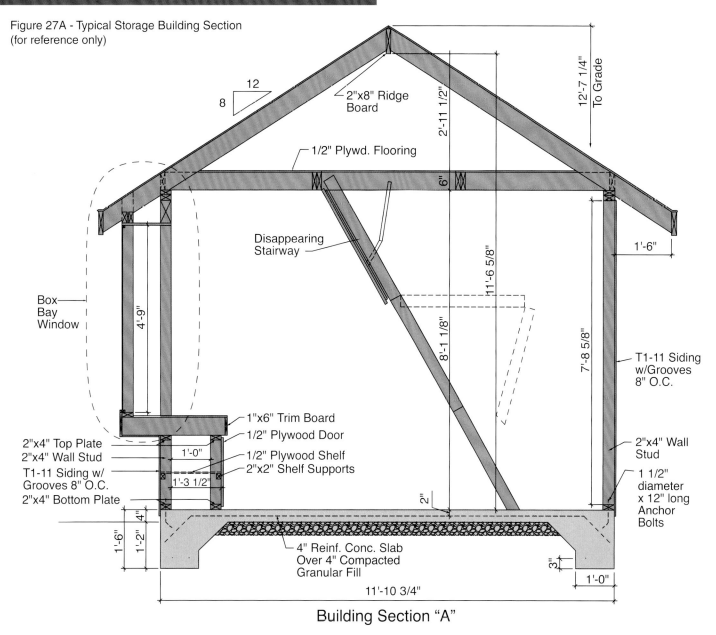

12
8

2"x8" Ridge Board

1/2" Plywd. Flooring

2'-11 1/2"

12'-7 1/4"
To Grade

6"

Disappearing Stairway

Box Bay Window

4'-9"

11'-6 5/8"

8'-1 1/8"

7'-8 5/8"

1'-6"

T1-11 Siding w/Grooves 8" O.C.

1"x6" Trim Board
1/2" Plywood Door
1/2" Plywood Shelf
2"x2" Shelf Supports

2"x4" Top Plate
2"x4" Wall Stud
T1-11 Siding w/ Grooves 8" O.C.
2"x4" Bottom Plate

1'-0"

1'-3 1/2"

2"

2"x4" Wall Stud

1 1/2" diameter x 12" long Anchor Bolts

4"

1'-6"

1'-2"

4" Reinf. Conc. Slab Over 4" Compacted Granular Fill

3"

1'-0"

11'-10 3/4"

Building Section "A"

Figure 27B - Typical Rafter Cutting Diagram

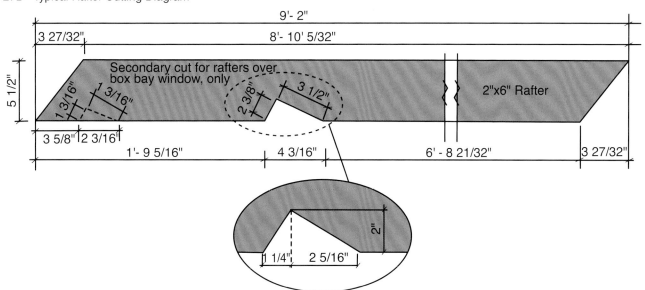

9'- 2"

3 27/32"

8'- 10' 5/32"

5 1/2"

Secondary cut for rafters over box bay window, only

1 3/16"

3/16"

2 3/8"

3 1/2"

2"x6" Rafter

3 5/8" 2 3/16"

1'- 9 5/16"

4 3/16"

6' - 8 21/32"

3 27/32"

2"

1 1/4" 2 5/16"

Roof Framing (continued)

Erecting the Rafters

Make sure the end rafters are plumb and that the ridge board is level and centered mid-span. Next, attach a diagonal brace between the ridge board and the 2x4 nailed to the top plate. Run the remaining rafters in pairs, attaching them to the ridge board first, then to the top plate (see Figures 28A and 28B). If your local codes require seismic/hurricane anchors, use metal connectors to secure the rafters to the top plate.

If a second ridge board is used, the process is repeated from the opposite end of the building. The junction of the ridge boards must be covered by two rafters. If you plan to install rafter ties (or ceiling joists), use three 16d nails to tie rafters to the rafter ties and cut the ties to match the slope of the rafters.

Be sure to add collar ties and hangers before removing any shoring or bracing.

Figure 28A - Ridge Board Supports

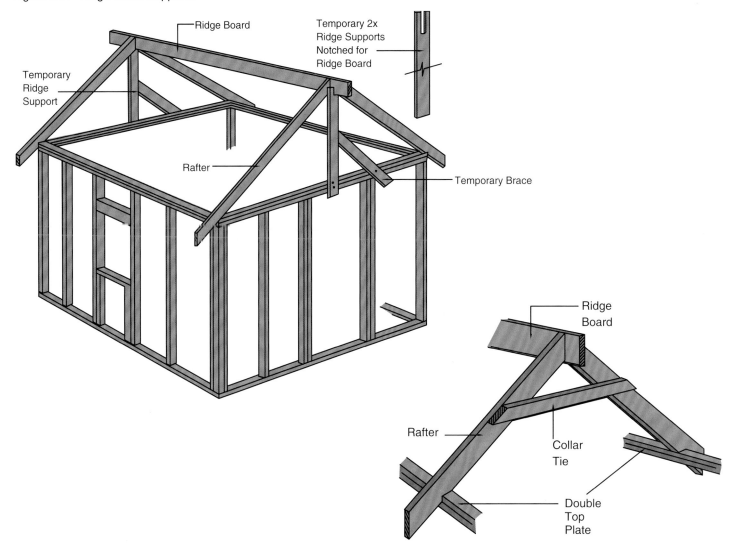

Figure 28B - Rafter Cuts

Using Metal Connectors For Framing

As mentioned earlier, metal fasteners provide the strength nails alone cannot provide. They also avoid the irritation of watching angled nails split the lumber that you have so carefully cut and fitted. Certain metal connectors allow the rafter to rest directly on the tie or top plate and eliminate the difficult and time-consuming bird's mouth cut (see Figure 29).

Other connectors are designed to join the rafter to the ridge board without toenailing. As you can see from the illustrations below, many different types of metal connectors are available for roof framing work. While metal roof framing connectors will add some additional expense to your project, they will save you time and create a more durable shed.

Figure 29 - Rafter Connector Examples

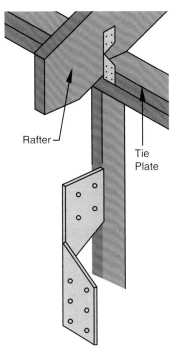

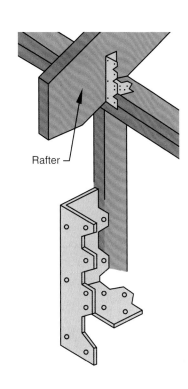

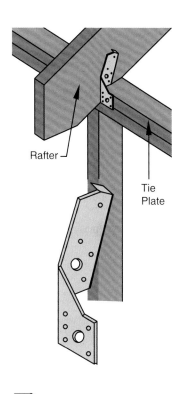

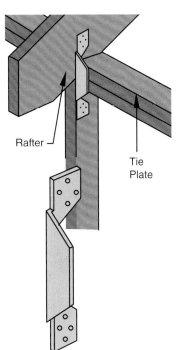

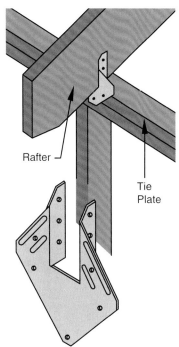

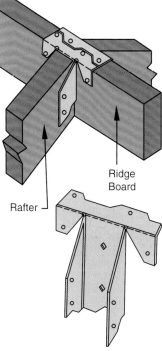

Variations of the Roof Cornice

Whatever type of roof you decide to construct, your building will have a roof overhang to protect the top of the side walls from moisture penetration. This overhang is generally known as the roof cornice. The cornice can also serve to provide ventilation and protection from the hot overhead rays of the sun on the sidewalls. As a general rule of thumb, warmer climates tend to favor longer overhangs that offer greater shading.

An open cornice is illustrated in Figure 30A. The overhang can extend up to 24" from the edge of the building. You have the option of adding a frieze board to the rafter ends or leaving the rafter ends exposed. Remember that when you create an exposed overhang, the roof sheathing is visible from underneath. Painting or staining the sheathing can improve its appearance.

Figure 30B represents a closed cornice. Make a seat cut on the rafter at the top plate. Cut the rafter ends flush and vertical with the top plate. Bring the siding all the way up to the rafters and finish off the cornice with a trim piece that covers the slightly exposed roof sheathing.

Two variations of the boxed cornice are shown in Figures 30C and 30D. A fascia board at the rafter ends is essential for any style of boxed cornice. Figure 30C demonstrates the sloping soffit design where the rafters are used to directly attach the soffit board. Nail a 1x fascia to the square cut rafter ends. Another frieze board covers the end portion of the soffit where it meets the wall siding.

Figure 30D portrays the level soffit design that requires 2x4 horizontal lookouts facenailed at the rafter ends and toenailed to wall siding. Level soffits generally extend no more than 12"-15" from the building wall. The lookouts help to frame the soffit construction.

Proper ventilation is essential for the boxed cornice. Install soffit vents (typically 4"x8") at regular intervals along the soffit between the lookouts. Be sure to install the screened vents or you will have unintentionally created a birdhouse wherever you have an unscreened vent!

Ventilation

If you plan to use your shed as a work area where you will spend longer periods of time, consider installing either gable end vents, or roof vents. Vents reduce interior temperatures during the summer and minimize condensation during the winter months. Gable end vents should be installed at both gable ends of your roof to promote cross-ventilation.

The number of roof vents you will install depends upon the cubic footage of your building. Simply create a box frame between roof rafters and install the vent according to the manufacturer's instructions. Don't forget to flash and then caulk the vent after you have installed the roof sheathing and shingles.

Figure 30A - Open Cornice

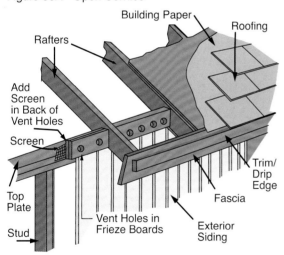

Figure 30B - Closed Cornice

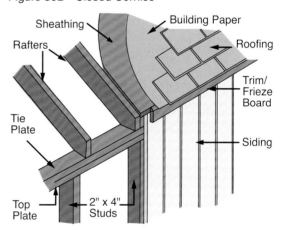

Figure 30C - Boxed Cornice/Sloping Soffit

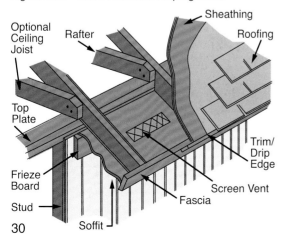

Figure 30D - Boxed Cornice/Level Soffit

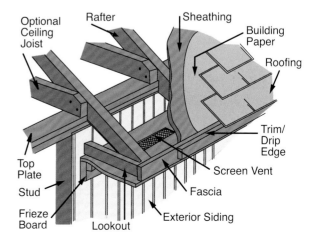

Roof Sheathing

Use 4'x8' plywood roof sheathing panels to create a strong base for your roofing material. The required thickness of sheathing will vary with rafter spacing and local building code requirements. Generally, the wider the rafter spacing, the thicker the sheathing needs to be. If you want the interior of your shed to have a finished building look, use 2x6 tongue and groove material to create a solid roof sheathing and paint the underside.

Stagger the sheathing, starting at the bottom, so that the end joints of adjacent sheets fall on different rafters. Space 6d nails 6" apart at sheet ends and 12" on center at intermediate rafters. Leave a 1/16" expansion gap between the ends of sheets. For larger jobs, you might want to rent a pneumatic staple gun to fasten sheathing. If gable eaves have an overhang, be certain to extend the sheathing to cover it.

Figure 31 - Plywood Sheathing Layout Plan

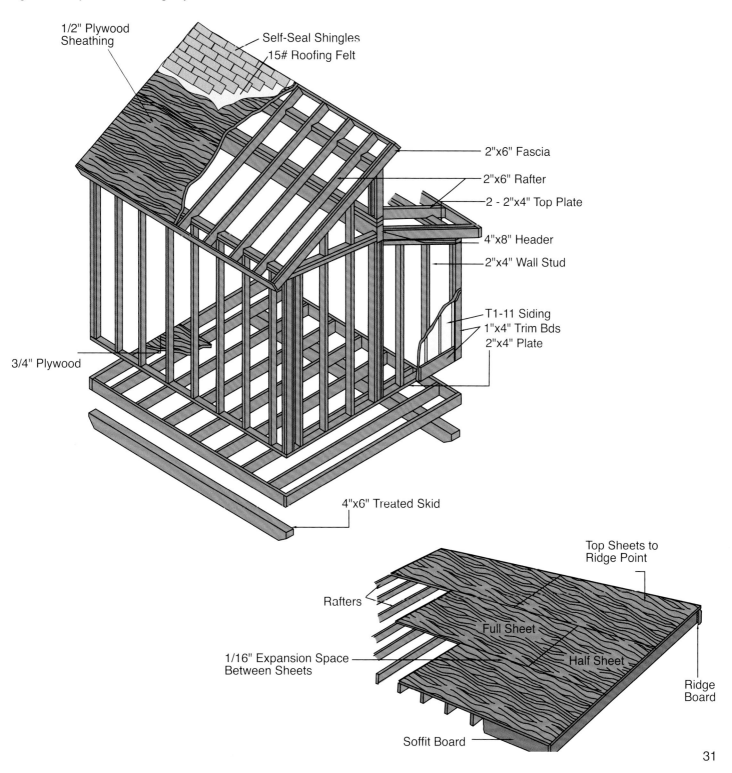

31

Gambrel Roof Construction

The gambrel roof offers an attractive barn-like alternative for your shed design. Construct a gambrel roof from trusses built on the ground and then erect the relatively lightweight trusses over the wall framing.

To add additional strength to your gambrel roof trusses in areas with heavy snow loads, use truss plate connectors and truss tie-down brackets to connect the truss to the top plate.

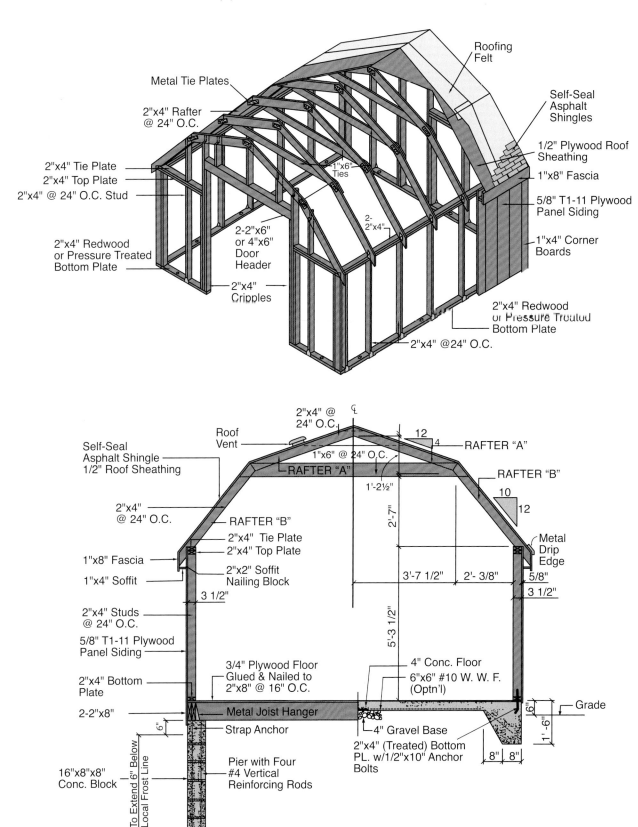

Metal Tie Plates

2"x4" Rafter @ 24" O.C.

2"x4" Tie Plate
2"x4" Top Plate
2"x4" @ 24" O.C. Stud

2"x4" Redwood or Pressure Treated Bottom Plate

2-2"x6" or 4"x6" Door Header

2"x4" Cripples

1"x6" Ties

2-2"x4"

Roofing Felt

Self-Seal Asphalt Shingles

1/2" Plywood Roof Sheathing
1"x8" Fascia

5/8" T1-11 Plywood Panel Siding

1"x4" Corner Boards

2"x4" Redwood or Pressure Treated Bottom Plate

2"x4" @24" O.C.

Self-Seal Asphalt Shingle
1/2" Roof Sheathing

Roof Vent

2"x4" @ 24" O.C.

1"x6" @ 24" O.C.

RAFTER "A"

RAFTER "A"

12 / 4

RAFTER "A"

RAFTER "B"

2"x4" @ 24" O.C.

RAFTER "B"

2"x4" Tie Plate
2"x4" Top Plate

1'-2½"

2'-7"

10 / 12

1"x8" Fascia

1"x4" Soffit

2"x2" Soffit Nailing Block

3 1/2"

Metal Drip Edge

5/8"

3 1/2"

3'-7 1/2"   2'- 3/8"

2"x4" Studs @ 24" O.C.

5/8" T1-11 Plywood Panel Siding

5'-3 1/2"

3/4" Plywood Floor Glued & Nailed to 2"x8" @ 16" O.C.

4" Conc. Floor
6"x6" #10 W. W. F. (Optn'l)

2"x4" Bottom Plate

2-2"x8"

Metal Joist Hanger

Strap Anchor

16"x8"x8" Conc. Block

To Extend 6" Below Local Frost Line

6"

Pier with Four #4 Vertical Reinforcing Rods

4" Gravel Base

2"x4" (Treated) Bottom PL. w/1/2"x10" Anchor Bolts

Grade

6"

1'-6"

8"   8"

TYPICAL SECTION

Shed Roof Construction

The shed roof lowers the height of one wall to create a lean-to appearance. Shed roofing is typical for buildings with clerestory windows (see Figure 33). The advantage of the shed roof and clerestory window combination is that without wall windows all of your wall space is available for storage but you still have plenty of natural light provided by the windows above your workspace.

Figure 33 - Section With Clerestory Lighting

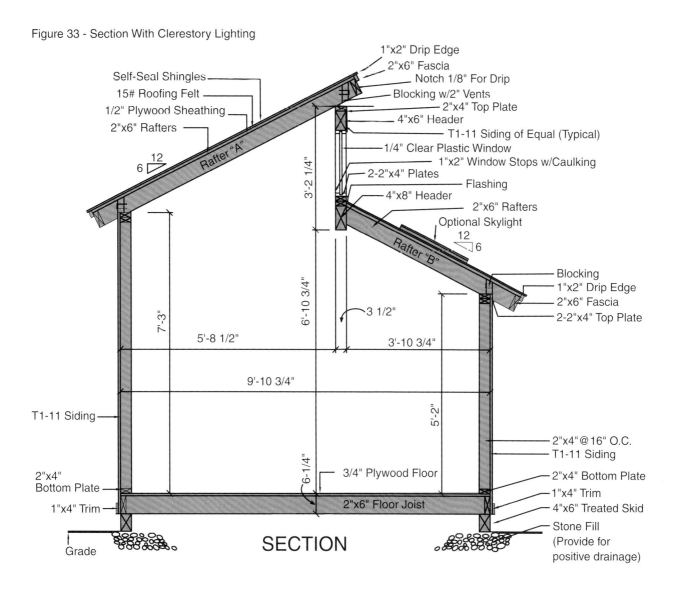

Self-Seal Shingles
15# Roofing Felt
1/2" Plywood Sheathing
2"x6" Rafters
Rafter "A"
12
6

1"x2" Drip Edge
2"x6" Fascia
Notch 1/8" For Drip
Blocking w/2" Vents
2"x4" Top Plate
4"x6" Header
T1-11 Siding of Equal (Typical)
1/4" Clear Plastic Window
1"x2" Window Stops w/Caulking
2-2"x4" Plates
Flashing
4"x8" Header
2"x6" Rafters
Optional Skylight
12
6
Rafter "B"

3'-2 1/4"

Blocking
1"x2" Drip Edge
2"x6" Fascia
2-2"x4" Top Plate

6'-10 3/4"

3 1/2"

7'-3"

5'-8 1/2"

3'-10 3/4"

9'-10 3/4"

5'-2"

T1-11 Siding

2"x4" @ 16" O.C.
T1-11 Siding

6-1/4"

3/4" Plywood Floor

2"x4"
Bottom Plate

2"x4" Bottom Plate
1"x4" Trim
4"x6" Treated Skid

1"x4" Trim

2"x6" Floor Joist

Stone Fill
(Provide for
positive drainage)

Grade

SECTION

Applying Vertical Panel Siding

Before starting construction, select the siding and determine the need for wall sheathing. Wall sheathing requirements are determined by the stud spacing, the width of the door and window jambs, and the application of the trim (see Figure 34A).

A common and inexpensive siding for sheds, T1-11 exterior siding does not require wall sheathing and adds structural strength. Flakeboard (Oriented Strand Board) is another inexpensive siding option for those with a tight budget. When you install vertical panel siding, nail 6d galvanized nails every 4"-6" at the edges of the panel and every 8"-12" inside the panel. You might be able to obtain siding nails that match the siding and thus eliminate painting

both the siding and nails. If you have to add a panel above the bottom panel, use Z-bar flashing between the panels (see Figure 34C). Leave a 1/4" gap around door and window openings when cutting siding to facilitate fitting.

When plywood sheathing is used, diagonal corner bracing can often be omitted. Decide whether trim is to be applied on top of the siding or butted into it. If butted, apply trim first, then apply siding. Horizontal wood siding is more expensive than plywood panel siding, but it provides an attractive and durable exterior. However, horizontal wood siding requires periodic painting for preservation.

Figure 34A - Siding Alternatives

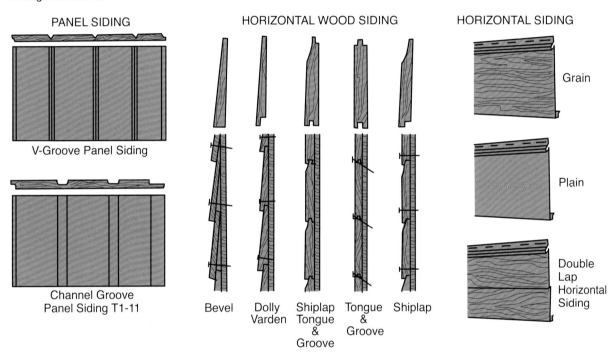

PANEL SIDING

V-Groove Panel Siding

Channel Groove
Panel Siding T1-11

HORIZONTAL WOOD SIDING

Bevel   Dolly Varden   Shiplap Tongue & Groove   Tongue & Groove   Shiplap

HORIZONTAL SIDING

Grain

Plain

Double Lap Horizontal Siding

Figure 34B - Panel Siding With Batten Boards

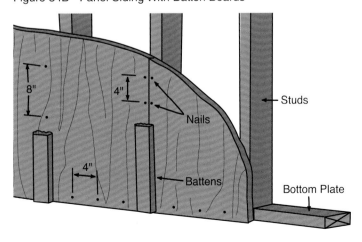

8"
4"
4"
Studs
Nails
Battens
Bottom Plate

Figure 34C - Vertical Grooved Siding Panels

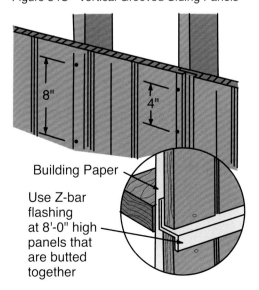

8"
4"
Building Paper
Use Z-bar flashing at 8'-0" high panels that are butted together

Applying Horizontal Hardboard Siding

Lay down various lengths of siding at each side. Apply so that joints in the succeeding course do not fall directly above each other. Butt all joints over the center of a stud. Seal by painting the edges with primer before butting. Start the bottom of the first course 1/2" below the bottom plate. Siding on all walls should be aligned and level and each course equally spaced. Be careful to determine the lap and exposure to the weather before applying the second and succeeding courses. Measure the distance to be covered and divide it by the desired exposure to get the total number of courses of siding (see Figure 35A). Carefully mark these spaces on the corners of each wall, taking into consideration the overlap of the siding. Run a chalk line from one mark to another, leaving a horizontal chalk line on the building paper as a guide. If you are not applying sheathing or building paper, chalk the wall studs directly. Apply the siding and keep it consistent by checking your level.

Final openings, where siding meets the soffit if applicable, can be closed with a piece of quarter round or shingle mould. Protect your shed by painting or staining it as soon as possible.

Figure 35A - Marking Siding Courses

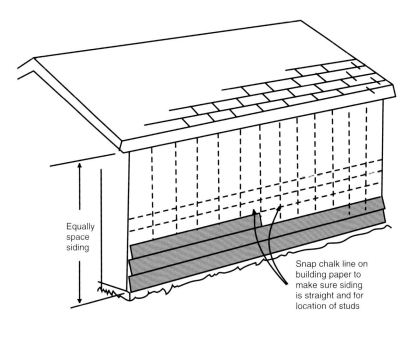

Equally space siding

Snap chalk line on building paper to make sure siding is straight and for location of studs

Figure 35B - Horizontal Siding Detail

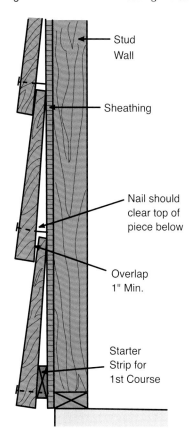

Stud Wall

Sheathing

Nail should clear top of piece below

Overlap 1" Min.

Starter Strip for 1st Course

Building Paper

Figure 35C Applying Building Paper

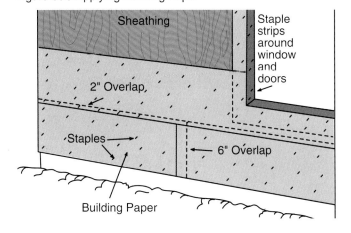

Sheathing

Staple strips around window and doors

2" Overlap

Staples

6" Overlap

Building Paper

Some local building codes might require that building paper be used to seal the wall from the elements. Building paper is typically felt or kraft paper impregnated with asphalt and is stapled or nailed between the siding and the sheathing or studs. Rolls are usually 36" wide and come in lengths between 200 to 500 square feet. Apply building paper in horizontal strips from the bottom of the wall as shown in Figure 35C. Overlaps should be 2" at horizontal joints, 6" at vertical joints, and 12" at corners. Cutting is done with a utility knife. Use just enough staples or nails in an installation to hold the paper in place. Siding nails will hold it permanently. Before you install siding, snap a level chalk line on the bottom of the paper and work up to keep the siding level.

Overhang Details

Before applying trim, know the nailing requirements of the siding you select. Some siding will have trim applied over the siding, but other types of siding will butt against trim and require extra blocking at the edges. After the roof sheathing is on, but before you install the fascia and rake boards, add soffit nailers if required. Use the longest fascia boards on the longest walls. Join all ends over the center of a rafter or nailer. Consult Figures 36A to 36F below. At the gable end, extend the fascia (or rake board) along the edge of the roof sheathing and rafter. At the top, cut the end to the angle of the rafter and butt at the center. Be sure to prime coat both ends before butting. At the lower end, let the front rake fascia extend beyond the side fascia, then cut the ends to line up with the side fascia.

Figure 36A - Boxed Cornice Detail

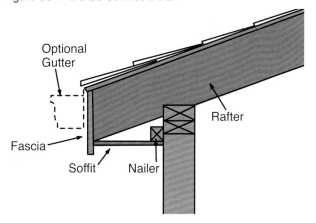

Figure 36B - Closed Cornice Detail

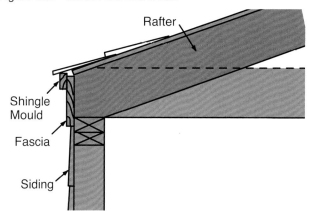

Figure 36C - Gable End Ridge Detail Box Overhang

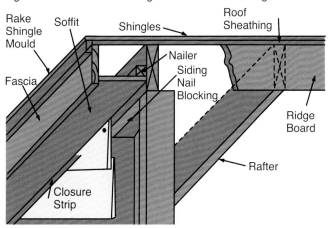

Figure 36D - Eave Detail Box Overhang

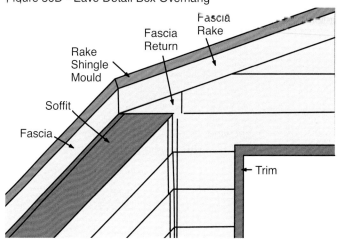

Figure 36E - Gable End Ridge Detail Open Overhang

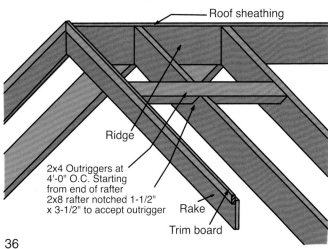

Figure 36F - Open Cornice Overhang

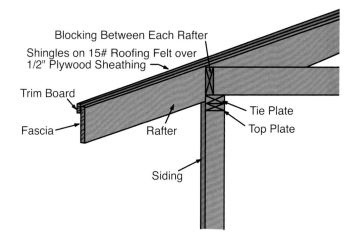

Corner Trim Details

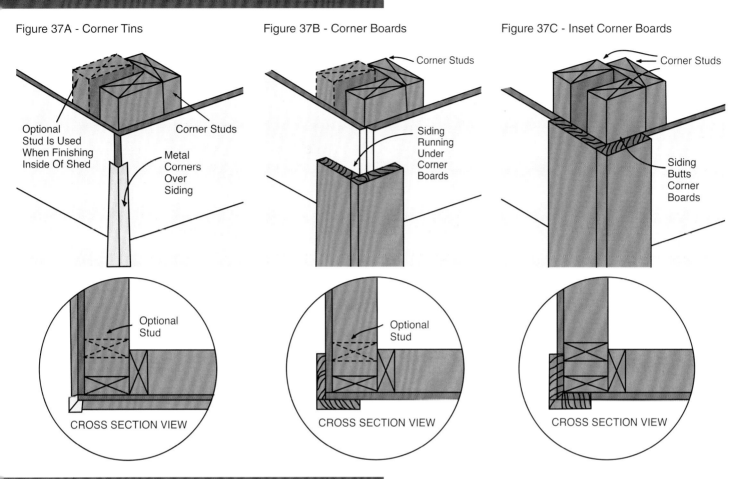

Figure 37A - Corner Tins

Optional Stud Is Used When Finishing Inside Of Shed

Corner Studs

Metal Corners Over Siding

Optional Stud

CROSS SECTION VIEW

Figure 37B - Corner Boards

Corner Studs

Siding Running Under Corner Boards

Optional Stud

CROSS SECTION VIEW

Figure 37C - Inset Corner Boards

Corner Studs

Siding Butts Corner Boards

CROSS SECTION VIEW

Window & Door Details

Study the typical window and door details shown in Figures 37D, 37E and Figures 38A, 38B for examples of door and window framing construction. Because of the great variety in window manufacturing, it is best to study the window manufacturer's installation instructions before framing and trimming them. Small sheds can utilize a built on-site door constructed from plywood and 1x trim (see Figure 37E). Other shed designs with greater traffic should use an exterior prehung door complete with threshold and side and head jambs (see Figures 37D and 38A).

Figure 38B illustrates the installation of a metal framed window with nail-on flange. These windows are inexpensive, readily available, and relatively easy to install. Consult the manufacturer's installation instructions for precise step-by-step procedures.

Figure 37D - Service Door Jamb Detail

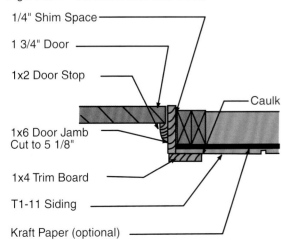

1/4" Shim Space

1 3/4" Door

1x2 Door Stop

Caulk

1x6 Door Jamb Cut to 5 1/8"

1x4 Trim Board

T1-11 Siding

Kraft Paper (optional)

Figure 37E - Built On-Site Barn Door

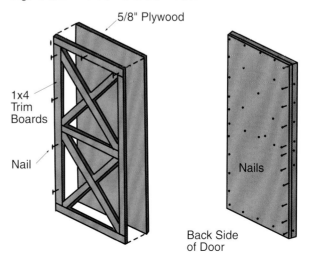

5/8" Plywood

1x4 Trim Boards

Nail

Nails

Back Side of Door

37

Figure 38A - Service Door Head

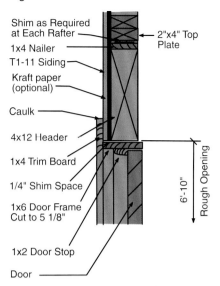

Shim as Required at Each Rafter
1x4 Nailer
T1-11 Siding
Kraft paper (optional)
Caulk
4x12 Header
1x4 Trim Board
1/4" Shim Space
1x6 Door Frame Cut to 5 1/8"
1x2 Door Stop
Door
2"x4" Top Plate
6'-10" Rough Opening

Figure 38B - Metal-Framed Window Installation

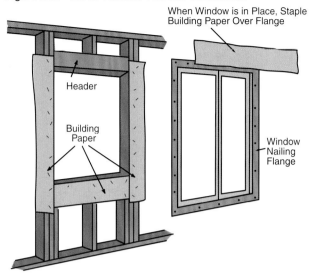

When Window is in Place, Staple Building Paper Over Flange
Header
Building Paper
Window Nailing Flange

Roof Shingles

Once the roof sheathing, cornice trim, and fascia boards are in place, the roof shingles can be applied. See the shingle manufacturer's instructions on the bundle. Shingles chosen to harmonize with or match your home are recommended. Square butt shingles are 36" x 12" in size, have three tabs, and are normally laid with 5" exposed to the weather (see Figure 38C).

Start with 15# asphalt felt paper at the bottom edge of the roof. Lap each course 2". After the roofing felt is on, apply a starter course of shingles (shingles turned upside down), lapping over the eave and rake fascia 1/2" to provide a drip edge. Use four nails for each shingle and apply a Boston ridge at top that is made by cutting a shingle into thirds (see Figure 38G). Start at one end of the ridge and fasten with two nails to a shingle leaving a 5" exposure. Cut shingles with a utility knife. Metal drip edges are used in some regions.

For a simple-to-install shed roof, use corrugated panel roofing (see Figure 38D). Be sure to overhang the eave by at least 2" and install a ridge cap. You can insert one or two translucent fiberglass roof panels between the solid metal roof panels to provide for natural lighting.

Figure 38C - Shingle Plan

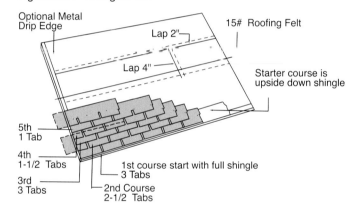

Optional Metal Drip Edge
Lap 2"
15# Roofing Felt
Lap 4"
Starter course is upside down shingle
5th 1 Tab
4th 1-1/2 Tabs
1st course start with full shingle
3 Tabs
3rd 3 Tabs
2nd Course 2-1/2 Tabs

Figure 38D - Panel Roofing

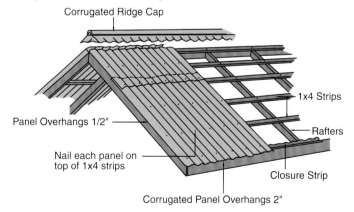

Corrugated Ridge Cap
1x4 Strips
Rafters
Panel Overhangs 1/2"
Nail each panel on top of 1x4 strips
Closure Strip
Corrugated Panel Overhangs 2"

Figure 38F - Tab Shingles

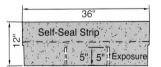

36"
Self-Seal Strip
12"
5" 5" Exposure

Tab shingles are always applied so that a full tab is centered over a slot below. If length of roof requires a narrow piece to finish first course, start the second row with piece of same width. Continue alternating narrow pieces in each succeeding row.

Figure 38G - Cutting A Shingle

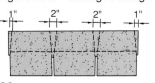

1" 2" 2" 1"

To cut a shingle, score a line with your utility knife, then bend and snap off the piece. Make 3 hip or ridge shingles from one shingle.

Figure 38E - Shingle Ridge Detail

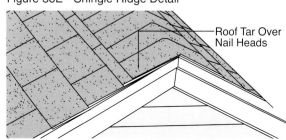

Roof Tar Over Nail Heads

Installing Electrical Wiring

Depending on how you are going to utilize your shed, you might want to install electrical wiring (see Figure 39). Two steps are mandatory if you plan to supply your shed with electrical service and want to do the job yourself:

1. First check with your local building department and determine the code standards for your area. They will advise you regarding permit and inspection requirements. They will also advise you whether or not there are any requirements for using a professional electrician during wiring.

2. Consult with your local power company. They will inform you if you need a separate electrical service for your shed. If you plan on running off of an existing home service, they will tell you if your home service can carry the additional load.

If you are allowed to use a branch circuit from your main panel, install an additional Ground Fault Circuit Interrupter (GFCI) type circuit breaker in your main circuit box and then use buried cable (Type UF cable for underground burial) to supply electricity to your shed. Bury the cable in an area that will not be disturbed by digging or other activity. Certain municipalities might not allow buried cable and will require a separate service installation.

You should install a main disconnect box for electrical service inside your shed. Be sure not to exceed the total amperage rating of the box in your branch circuits. Inside the shed, you can wire lighting and receptacles using either romex (Type NM cable) or metal sheathed cable (Type BX cable) depending upon your local code requirements. If you are wiring a moist area such as a greenhouse or cabana, use Type NMC cable or Type UM for extra protection against moisture. Also install GFCI receptacles in areas with excessive moisture. Consult your local building department for GFCI requirements and regulations.

Figure 39 - Electrical Wiring Options

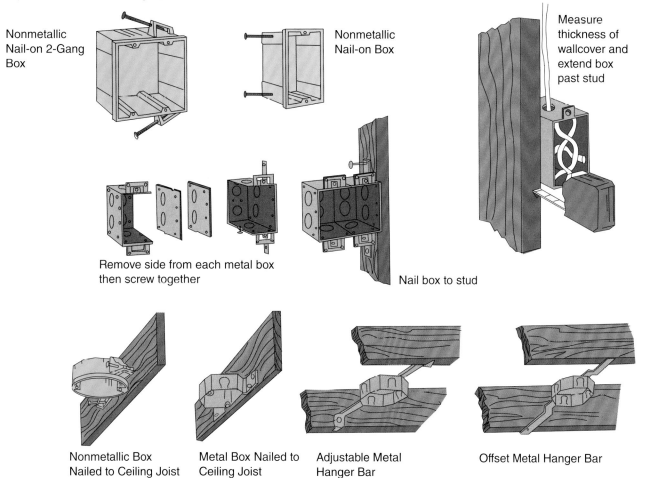

Nonmetallic Nail-on 2-Gang Box

Nonmetallic Nail-on Box

Measure thickness of wallcover and extend box past stud

Remove side from each metal box then screw together

Nail box to stud

Nonmetallic Box Nailed to Ceiling Joist

Metal Box Nailed to Ceiling Joist

Adjustable Metal Hanger Bar

Offset Metal Hanger Bar

Finishing the Inside of Your Shed

You can either finish the interior of your shed with drywall or leave the wall studs exposed and use blocking to build shelving between the studs. Most storage shed builders will want to take advantage of the extra storage space afforded by the open wall sections. Use your imagination to create additional storage space by nailing or screwing 1x2 cleats to the studs and then installing extended horizontal shelving over the cleats.

If you elect to install 4'x8' drywall panels (also known as wallboard) in your shed, study the illustration below for suggestions on nailing or gluing drywall to wall studs.

A variety of fasteners are available for wallboard. Consult your local home improvement store, or building material supplier for suggestions. After you have installed the panels, you can tape and fill the joints with joint compound or simply cover the joints with tape if the final appearance is not a major concern.

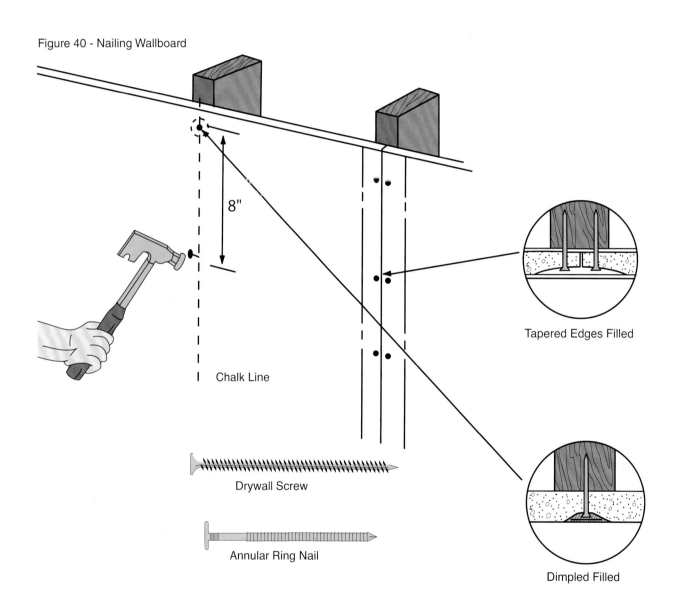

Figure 40 - Nailing Wallboard

8"

Chalk Line

Drywall Screw

Annular Ring Nail

Tapered Edges Filled

Dimpled Filled

Adding a Ramp to Your Shed

An entry ramp makes life easier for you and your shed. Instead of lugging heavy garden tools such as mowers or snow removal machines up and down from ground level to shed level, use a ramp built from solid 2x material to improve accessibility. If your ramp will be over 3 feet in width, add an additional 2x vertical support to the center of the ramp. Nail the ramp decking to the ramp supports with 12d hot-dipped galvanized nails or use 3" decking screws.

Figure 41A - Design A

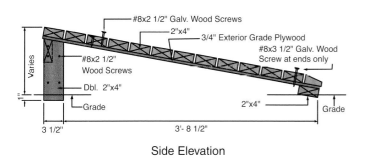

Side Elevation

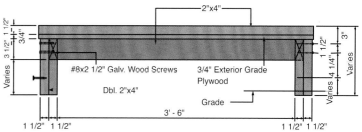

Back Side Elevation

Figure 41B - Design B

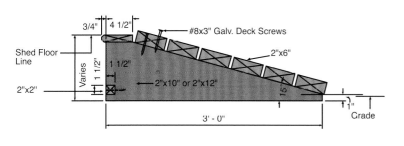

Side Elevation

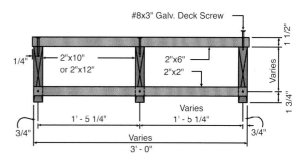

Back Side Elevation

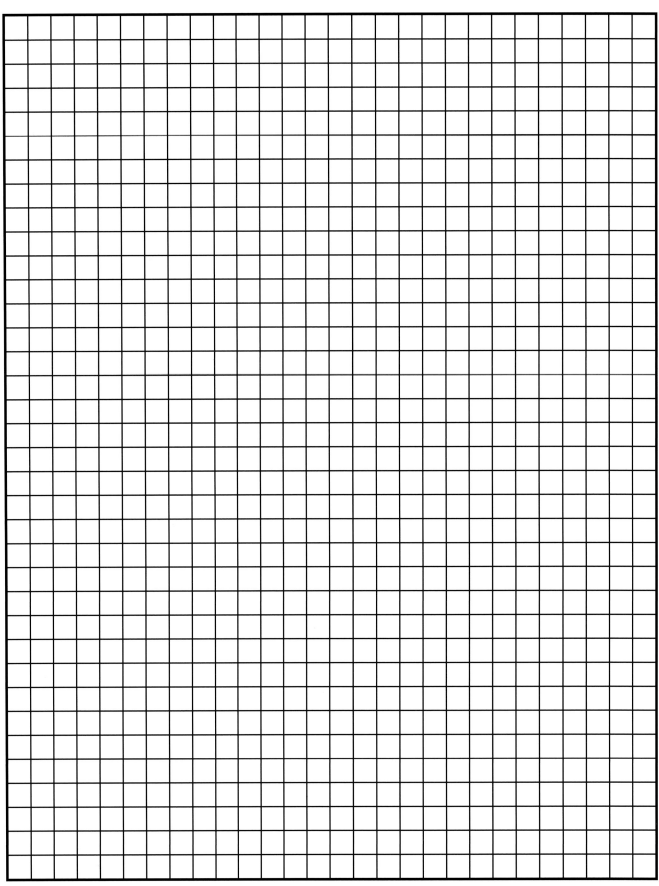

Scale: ¼" = 1'-0" per square

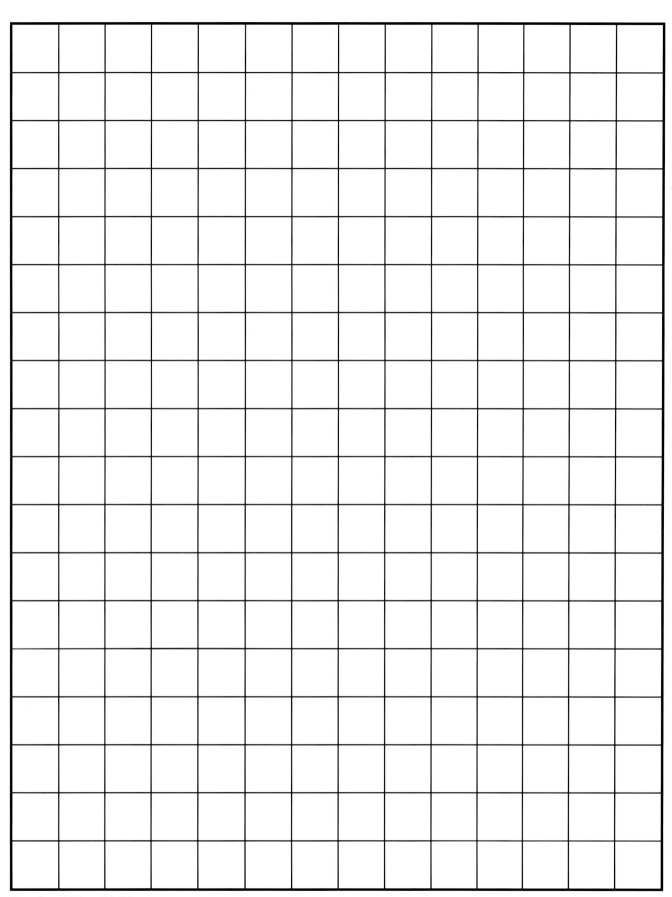

Scale: ½" = 1'-0" per square

Glossary

Anchor Bolt - A metal connector device used to connect a wood mudsill to a concrete wall or slab.

Batterboards - Scrap lumber nailed horizontally to stakes driven near each corner of the foundation excavation. Stretch nylon strings between batterboards to transfer reference points and to measure elevation.

Beam - Beams are horizontal structural members that are supported by vertical posts. Beams are typically constructed from 2 or more 2-bys, 4-by material, or engineered lumber.

Bottom Plate - In stud wall framing, the bottom horizontal member of the wall. Also known as the soleplate.

Bridging - Wood or metal cross pieces fastened between floor joists to provide structural strength.

Cantilever - Refers to the end portion of a joist that extends beyond the beam.

Casing - Molding around door and window openings.

Codes - Regulations implemented by your local building department which control the design and construction of buildings and other structures. Consult your local building department for applicable codes before you begin your construction project.

Collar Beam - A connecting member used between rafters to strengthen the roof structure.

Cornice - The structure created at the eave overhang which typically consists of fascia board, soffit, and moldings.

Cripple Studs - Short studs that strengthen window and door openings or the gable end of a roof. Also known as jack studs.

Defect - Any defect in lumber whether a result of a manufacturing imperfection or an irregularity in the timber from which the lumber was cut. Some defects are only blemishes while others can reduce strength and durability. Grading rules establish the extent and severity of wood defects.

Drip Edge - Angled metal or wood located on the outer edge of the roof. Drip edge prevents water penetration.

Drywall - A gypsum panel used to finish interior walls. Also known as plasterboard or sheet rock.

Eave - The roof overhang projecting beyond the exterior wall.

Edge - The narrowest side of a piece of lumber which is perpendicular to both the face and the end.

Elevation - Drawing of a structure as it will appear from the front, rear, left and right sides.

Engineered Lumber - Refers to beams or rafters constructed from wood fiber and glue such as glu-lams, micro-lams, or wood I-beams. Often superior in strength and durability to dimensional lumber.

Face - The widest side of a piece of lumber which is perpendicular to both the edge and the end.

Fascia - Trim used along the eave or gable end.

Finish - Any protective coating applied to your structure to protect against weathering. Finishes are available as stains, paints, or preservatives.

Flakeboard - A panel material made from compressed wood chips bonded with resin. Also known as oriented strand board (OSB) or chipboard.

Flashing - Metal material used on the roof and eaves to prevent moisture penetration.

Fly Rafters - Rafters at the gable end which "fly" unsupported by the tie plate. Also known as rack, barge, or verge rafters.

Footing - Concrete footings help to anchor your foundation or piers in the surrounding soil and distribute weight over a larger surface area. In climates where the soil freezes, a generous footing protects against soil heaves and structural slippage.

Frieze - A horizontal framing member that connects the siding with the soffit.

Frost Line - Measure of the maximum penetration of frost in the soil in a given geographic location. Depth of frost penetration varies with climate conditions.

Furring - Narrow strips of wood attached to walls or other surfaces that serve as a fastening base for drywall.

Gable - The triangular end of the roof structure formed by the roof framing.

Galvanized Nails - Hot-dipped galvanized nails (HDG) are dipped in zinc and will not rust.

Girder - Same as beam.

Grade Stamp - A stamp imprinted on dimensional lumber which identifies wood species, grade, texture, moisture content, and usage. Grade descriptions such as select, finish, and common signify limiting characteristics that may occur in lumber in each grade. The stamp indicates a uniform measurement of performance that permits lumber of a given grade to be used for the same purpose, regardless of the manufacturer.

Grading - The process of excavating, leveling, and compacting the soil or gravel beneath your foundation to its desired finish level. Proper grading avoids drainage problems.

Grain - Lumber shows either a flat or vertical grain depending on how it was cut from the log. To minimize warping along the face of decking (known as cupping) and raising of the grain, you should place flat grain decking with the bark side up or facing out.

Header - A horizontal load-bearing support member over an opening in the wall such as window or door openings.

Heartwood - Core of the log that resists decay.

Hip Rafter - A short rafter that forms the hip of a roof and runs from the corner of a wall to the ridge board. Usually set at a 45-degree angle to the walls.

Jack Rafter - A short rafter that runs from the ridge board to a hip or valley rafter or from the hip rafter to the tie plate.

Joist - Lumber which is set on edge and supports a floor, decking, or ceiling. Joists in turn are supported by beams and posts.

Joist Hanger - A metal connector available in many sizes and styles that attaches to a ledge or rim joist and makes a secure butt joint between ledger and joist.

Lag Screw - Heavy-duty fastener with hexagonal bolt head that provides extra fastening power for critical structural connections. Use galvanized lag screws to prevent rust.

Glossary

Ledger - A horizontal support member to which joists or other support members are attached.

Let-in Brace - Usually a 1x4 corner brace in a wall section that runs diagonally from the bottom to top plate.

Look-out - Blocking which extends from an inner common rafter to the fly rafters at the gable ends.

Metal Connectors - Used to augment or replace nails as fasteners, metal connectors are critical for lasting and sturdy garage construction.

Moisture Content - Moisture content of wood is the weight of water in wood expressed as a percentage of the weight of wood from which all water has been removed. The drier the lumber the less the lumber will shrink and warp. Surfaced lumber with a moisture content of 19% or less is known as dry lumber and is typically grade stamped as "S-DRY." Moisture content over 19% results in a "S-GRN" stamp to indicate surfaced green.

Mudsill - The part of the wall framing that contacts the foundation. Should be pressure-treated to resist moisture and decay. Also known as the sill plate.

Outrigger - An extension of a rafter at the eave used to form a cornice or overhang on a roof.

Pea Gravel - Approximately 1/4" round gravel material used in a 4"-6" layer to cover the soil under your concrete slab.

Perpendicular - At a 90 degree or right angle.

Pilot Hole - A slightly undersized hole drilled in lumber which prevents splitting of the wood when nailed.

Pitch - A measurement of roof slope. Expressed as the ratio of the total rise divided by the span.

Plumb - Absolutely vertical. Determined with either a plumb bob or spirit level.

Post - A vertical support member which bears the weight of the joists and beams. Typically posts are at least 4x4 lumber.

Pressure-treated - Refers to the process of forcing preservative compounds into the fiber of the wood. Handle pressure-treated lumber with caution and do not inhale or burn its sawdust. Certain types of pressure-treated lumber are suitable for ground contact use while others must be used above ground. While more expensive than untreated lumber, pressure-treated wood resists decay and is recommended where naturally decay-resistant species like cedar or redwood are unavailable or too costly.

Purlin - A horizontal member of the roof framing that supports rafters or spans between trusses.

Rafter - A roof framing member that extends from the top plate to the ridge board and supports the roof sheeting and roofing material.

Rake - The inclined end area of a gable roof.

Redwood - Decay-resistant and stable wood for exterior use. Heartwood grades provide the greatest decay resistance.

Reinforcing Bar - A steel rod which provides internal reinforcement for concrete piers and foundations. Also known as rebar.

Ridge Board - A 1x or typically 2x member on edge at the roof's peak to which the rafters are connected.

Right Triangle, 6-8-10 or 3-4-5 - A means of ensuring squareness when you lay out your foundations. Mark a vertical line at exactly 8'-0" from the angle you want to square. Then mark a horizontal line at exactly 6'-0" from the crossing vertical line. Measure the distance diagonally between both the 6'-0" and 8'-0" marks and when the distance measures 10'-0" exactly you have squared a 90 degree angle between lines.

Rise - In roof construction the vertical distance the ridge rises above the top plate at the center of the span.

Rough Sill - The lowest framing member of a door or window opening.

Scale - A system of representation in plan drawing where small dimensions represent an equivalent large dimension. Most construction plans are said to be scaled down. Scale is expressed as an equation such as 1/4"=1'-0".

Screed - A straight piece of lumber used to level wet concrete or the gravel.

Sheathing - Exterior sheet (typically 4'x8') material fastened to the rafter or exterior stud walls.

Slope - A measurement of inclination and is expressed as a percentage of units of vertical rise per units of horizontal distance.

Soffit - The underside of the roof overhang. Soffits can either be closed or open (thus exposing the roof rafters).

Span - The distance between two opposing walls as measured from the outside of the top plates or the distance between two beam supports which is measured from center to center.

Spirit Level - A sealed cylinder with a transparent tube nearly filled with liquid forming a bubble used to indicate true vertical and horizontal alignment when the bubble is centered in the length of the tube.

String Level - A spirit level mounted in a frame with prongs at either end for hanging on a string. Determines level across string lines.

Stud - The vertical framing member of a wall.

T1-11 Siding - Exterior siding material with vertical grooves usually 8" on center.

Tie Plate - The framing member nailed to the top plates in order to connect and align wall sections. Also known as the cap plate or second top plate.

Toenail - To drive a nail at an angle. When you toenail a post to a beam for example, drive the nail so that one-half the nail is in each member.

Top Plate - The horizontal top part of the wall framing perpendicular to the wall studs.

Tongue and Groove - Refers to the milling of lumber so that adjacent parts interlock for added strength and durability.

Trimmer Stud - The stud adjacent to window or door opening studs which strengthens the opening and bears the weight of the window or door headers. Also known as a jack stud.

Truss - A triangular prefabricated unit for supporting a roof load over a span. Trusses are relatively lightweight and can offer an easier method of roof construction for the novice.

Valley Rafter - A rafter running from a tie plate at the corner of a wall along the roof valley and up to the ridge.

Ready to Start Some Serious Planning?

Now that you have read this do-it-yourself manual, you're ready to start some serious planning. As you can see, there are many details to consider, and they all tie together for successful completion of your shed project.

If the instructions appear at first confusing, reread the information outlined in this book several times before deciding which phases of construction you want to handle yourself and which might require professional assistance.

Because drawing up your own plan from scratch can be time consuming and difficult for the inexperienced builder, you might want to make planning and cost estimating easier by selecting a shed, or other outdoor project plan shown in this book.

Often blueprints with material lists are not readily available from your local building material store, but you can order a shed, an outbuilding, or an outdoor project plan from this book that includes a material list (see specific plan for availability). If, after reviewing the blueprints you still have questions, talk them over with your local lumber dealer. Most dealers are familiar with construction and will be glad to help you.

This book includes a large assortment of shed plans, larger sheds, and other outdoor projects. Remember that construction blueprints can be ordered for all of these projects by mailing the order form on page 164, visiting houseplansandmore.com, or by calling 1-800-373-2646.

Example of a Typical Project Plan Sheet

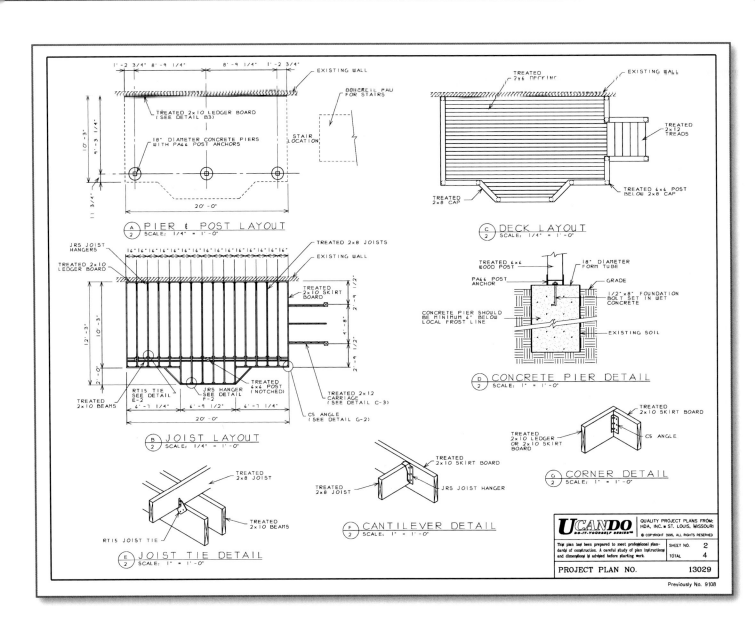

Shed Plans

Plan #F55-002D-4506 on page 59

Our collection of do-it-yourself shed plans features a wide variety of shed designs including garden sheds, workshops and more. Building a shed will make maintaining a well-kept yard so much easier because all your yard equipment and tools will be readily available. All of these shed plans are easy-to-build and will be the perfect complement to your home and yard.

The Boscobel Garden Shed Plan

The Boscobel garden shed is absolutely the perfect garden shed thanks to plenty of light in the interior. Ceiling and wall windows flood the inside with warm, natural sunlight. This shed will become the ideal place for seedlings to flourish in colder temperatures, or the perfect spot to cultivate new plants for your very own organic gardening area. This is a wonderful complement to any backyard and offers plenty of windows for year-round gardening.

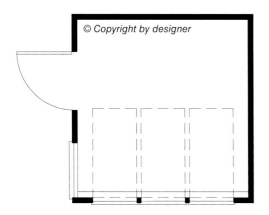

© Copyright by designer

PLAN #F55-002D-4523

- Size - 10' x 10'
- 100 square feet
- Wood floor on 4x4 runners
- Building height - 11'-3 1/2"
- Left wall height - 8'
- Material list included
- Step-by-step instructions included

PLAN #F55-002D-4523
MATERIAL LIST

QTY.	SIZE	DESCRIPTION
FLOOR FRAMING		
1/4 cubic yard		Gravel
4 pcs.	4x4x10' treated	Floor runners
2 pcs.	2x4x10' treated	Band boards
11 pcs.	2x4x10' treated	Floor joists
22 pcs.	5/4x6x10' treated	Floor decking
WALL FRAMING		
40 pcs.	2x4x7'-8 5/8" (pre-cut)	Wall studs
16 pcs.	2x4x10'	Wall plates
1 pc.	2x6x8'	Wall headers
1 pc.	2x8x10'	Plant shelf
ROOF FRAMING		
1 pc.	2x8x12'	Ridge board
6 pcs.	2x6x12'	Rafters
13 pcs.	2x6x10'	Rafters
1 pc.	2x6x10'	Blocking
2 pcs.	2x4x8'	Collar ties
6 shts.	4x8x1/2" ext. plywood	Roof sheathing
DOOR, WINDOWS, LOUVERS AND RAMP		
1 ea.	3'-0"x6'-8"	15 Lite door
2 ea.	10/12x4'-0" base	Wood louvers (optional)
24 pcs.	3/4"x3/4"x10'	Window frame
3 shts.	3'x7'x1/4"	Plexiglass (cut to fit)
1 sht.	3'x8'x1/4"	Plexiglass (cut to fit)
3 shts.	3'x3'x1/4"	Plexiglass (cut to fit)
2 pcs.	1x6x10'	Window trim
9 pcs.	1x4x10'	Window trim
7 pcs.	1x2x8'	Window trim
7 pcs.	2x6x8' treated	Ramp
FINISH AND TRIM		
4 bundles	-	Asphalt shingles
1 roll	-	15# Roofing felt
6 pcs.	4 1/2"x10'	Metal drip edge
24 l.f.	10"	Metal flashing
260 l.f.	12"	Tri-lap hardboard siding
3 pcs.	1x4x8'	Door trim
7 pcs.	1x4x8'	Corner boards
1 pc.	1x6x8'	Corner boards
5 pcs.	1x8x12'	Fascia boards
4 pcs.	1x3x12'	Trim boards
1 sht.	4x8x3/8" ext. plywood	Soffit
4 tubes	-	Silicone
2 gal.	-	Ext. paint or stain/sealer
MISC. HARDWARE		
12 lbs.	16d	Cement coated nails
5 lbs.	8d	Cement coated nails
5 lbs.	8d	Galvanized nails
3 lbs.	6d	Galvanized nails
3 lbs.	7/8"	Roofing nails
1 lb.	3"	Galvanized screws
8 lbs.	2"	Galvanized screws
3 lbs.	1 1/2"	Galvanized screws
2 pcs.	11'-4"	T-type metal wall bracing

1. Study the plan thoroughly and read all instructions before starting the construction of the garden shed. Be sure to check your local code requirements and obtain a building permit if necessary.

SITE PREPARATION AND RUNNER PLACEMENT

2. Select a location that is level and slightly larger than the garden shed.

3. Dig (4) trenches approximately 8" wide, 11'-0" long, and 2" deep as shown in the details A and B. Fill each trench with gravel to the top of the grade. Packing or rolling the gravel will result in a more level base.

4. Cut (4) treated 4x4 runners 10'-0" long. Miter both ends of the 4x4's as shown in the detail C. Position the runners on the gravel trenches and ensure that they are square by measuring the corners. Diagonal dimensions should equal 14'-1 3/4". See detail B.

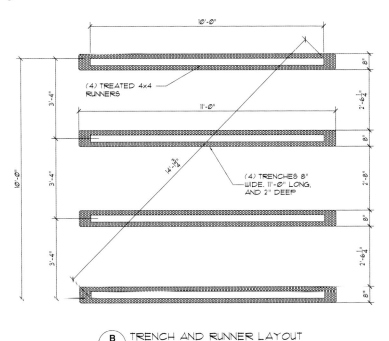

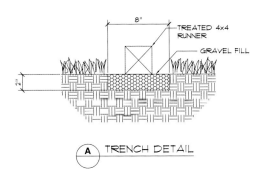

A TRENCH DETAIL

B TRENCH AND RUNNER LAYOUT

FLOOR FRAMING

5. Select (2) treated 2x4's 10'-0" long to use as band boards. Cut (11) treated 2x4 floor joists 9'-9" long. Nail the band boards to the joists using (2) 16d cc (16 penny cement coated) nails per joist at each end as shown in detail D.

6. Position the 2x4 floor framing on the 4x4 runners. Toenail 16d cc nails through each side of the 2x4 joists into the 4x4's.

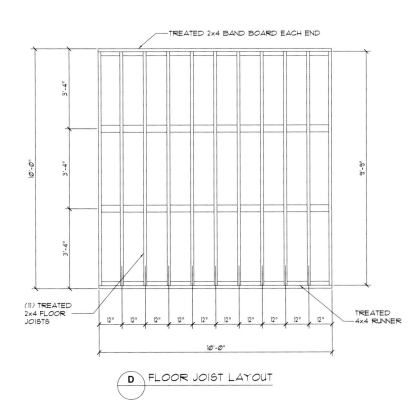

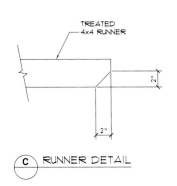

C RUNNER DETAIL

D FLOOR JOIST LAYOUT

7. Check to ensure floor system is level and square.

8. Fasten 5/4x6 treated decking to the 2x4 floor using (2) 2" screws per joist as shown in detail E. When spacing the boards, remember the boards will shrink slightly over a period of time. Lay the planks "bark side up" so that the rings curve down to avoid cupping and splitting. See detail F. Pre-drilling holes slightly smaller than the screws may also avoid splitting the wood.

WALL FRAMING

9. Use the deck floor as a work surface to construct the walls.

10. Door and vent rough opening dimensions may vary with that of the manufacturer. Verify rough opening sizes prior to fabricating walls.

11. Cut 2x4 studs, plates, and headers for the (4) wall panels as listed below.

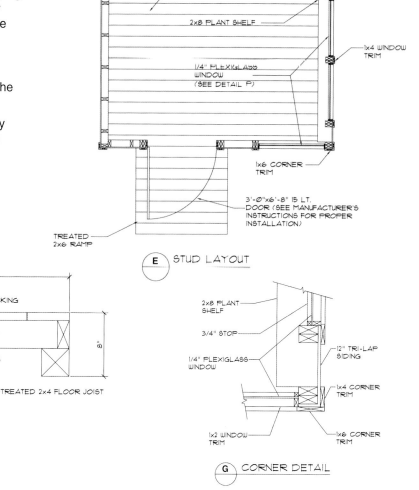

Qty.	Studs Length		Qty.	Plates Length		Qty.	Headers Length
(20)	7'-8 5/8" (pre-cut)		(3)	10'-0"		(2)	3'-5 1/2" (2x6)
(1)	7'-7 3/4" *		(3)	9'-5"			
(1)	6'-7 5/8" *		(2)	8'-3"			**Plant Shelf**
(1)	5'-6 1/4" *		(2)	6'-8 1/2"		**Qty.**	**Length**
(1)	5'-3" *		(2)	6'-5"		(1)	9'-6" (2x8)
(4)	5'-5 5/8"		(2)	4'-8 1/2" **			
(8)	5'-2 5/8"		(4)	3'-10 7/8" ***			
(3)	2'-7 1/2"		(1)	2'-10 1/2"			
(10)	8 1/2"		(3)	2'-5"			
			(4)	1'-1 1/2"			

   * = miter one end at 50 degrees.

  ** = miter both ends at 40 degrees.

 *** = miter both ends at 50 degrees.

12. Assemble the (4) wall panels as shown below, detail H. Nail the 2x4 top and bottom plates to the studs using (2) 16d cc nails per stud at each end. Attach the headers in the same manner. Secure metal wall bracing or 1x4 boards using 8d cc nails. See bracing detail J on page 53.

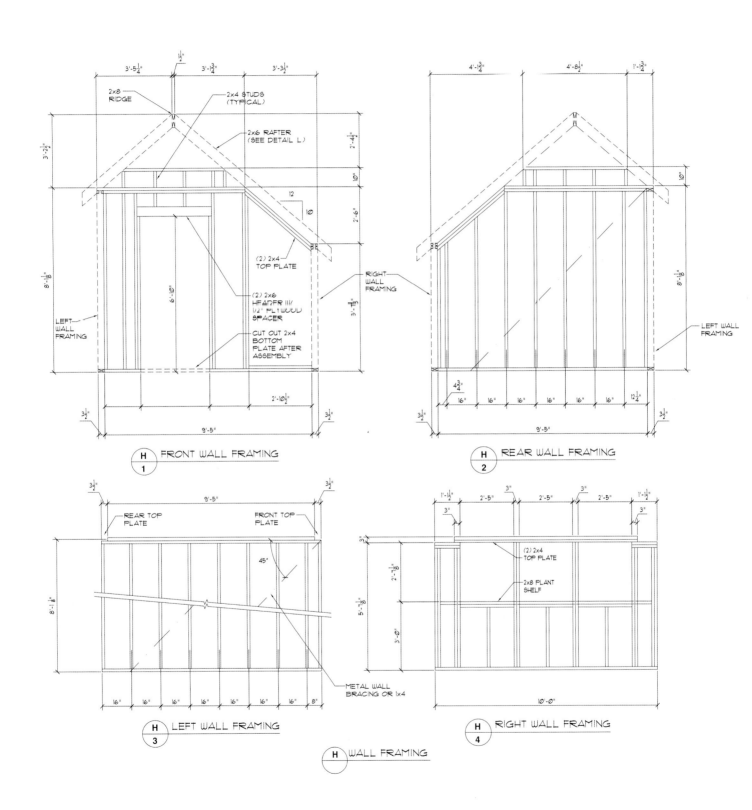

ERECTING THE WALLS

13. Position the wall panels in place on the deck floor as shown in detail I. Temporary bracing may be necessary. Making sure the walls are plumb and square, secure the wall panels to the floor using 16d cc nails. Nail the panels together at the corners. Cut 2x8 plant shelf to fit and nail in place.

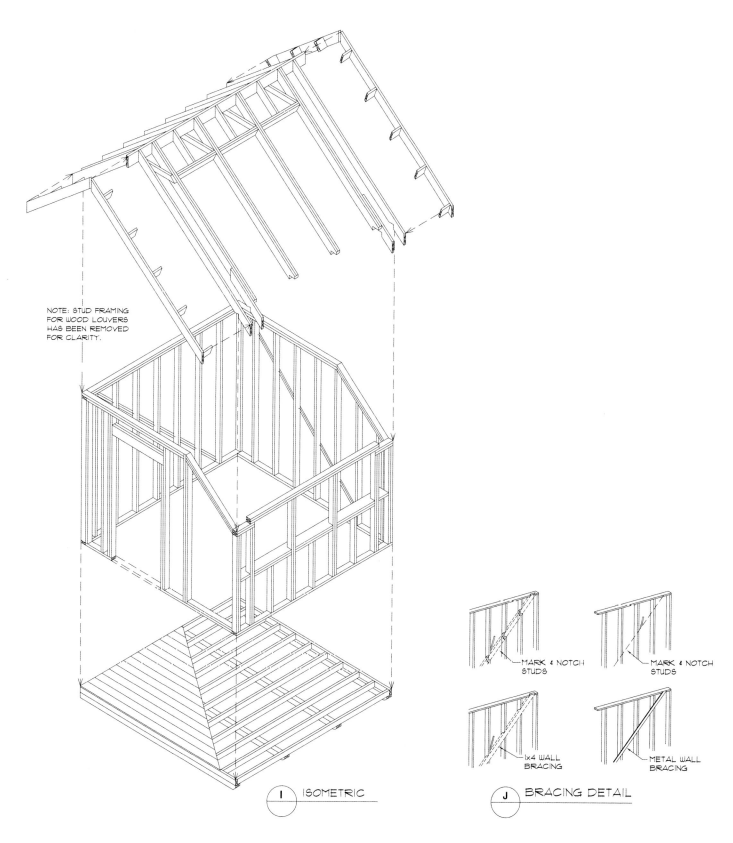

NOTE: STUD FRAMING FOR WOOD LOUVERS HAS BEEN REMOVED FOR CLARITY.

MARK & NOTCH STUDS

MARK & NOTCH STUDS

1x4 WALL BRACING

METAL WALL BRACING

I ISOMETRIC

J BRACING DETAIL

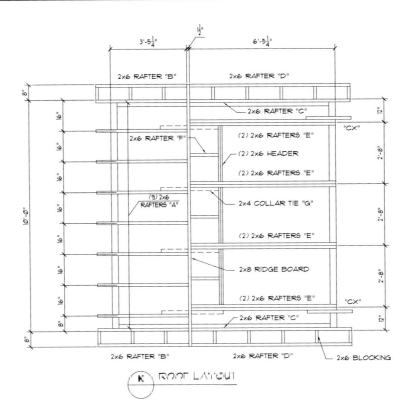

K ROOF LAYOUT

ROOF FRAMING

14. Cut (1) 2x8 ridge board 11'-4" long, (16) 2x6 blocks 6 1/2" long, and (6) 2x6 headers 2'-5" long.

15. Set the 2x8 ridge board as indicated in detail H1 and K using temporary bracing. Mark the top plates on the left and right walls for the location of the rafters.

16. Cut (1) "A", "C", and "E" rafter as shown in detail L. Set the boards in place to see if any adjustments need to be made. Use the rafters as templates to cut the remaining boards.

17. Assemble the roof as shown in details I and K using 16d cc nails. Cut and bevel (3) 2x4 blocks to fit between 2x6 rafters at the right wall. See detail M.

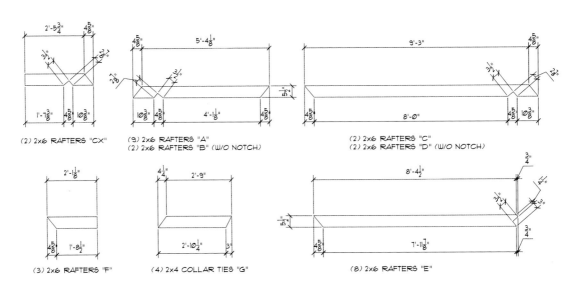

L RAFTER DETAIL

ROOF PLYWOOD

18. Measure and cut 1/2" plywood allowing a 3/4" overhang at all edges of the roof to cover the 1x8 fascia board as shown in detail M. Hold the plywood back 1 1/2" exposing the inside 2x6 rafter around the window opening for the 1/4" plexiglass to rest on. See details N and O. Fasten the plywood to the rafters with 8d cc nails spaced 6" apart.

WINDOW FRAMING

19. Glue and screw 3/4" window frame together with 1 1/2" galvanized screws to support the 1/4" plexiglass. Set the frames in place flush with the top of the rafters at the roof and 1 1/8" in from the outside of the front and right walls. See details M, N, and O. Screw the 3/4" frame in place using 1 1/2" screws. Pre-drilling holes may avoid splitting the wood.

20. Cut the 1/4" plexiglass to fit the window openings. Run a bead of clear silicone around the exposed 2x6 rafter and set the plexiglass in place on the roof. Run a second bead of silicone around the outside perimeter of the glass. Apply 1x4 and beveled 1x6 window trim to the roof. Pre-drill holes through the trim and plexiglass to avoid splitting. Apply a bead of silicone at the corners where the plexiglass and trim meet.

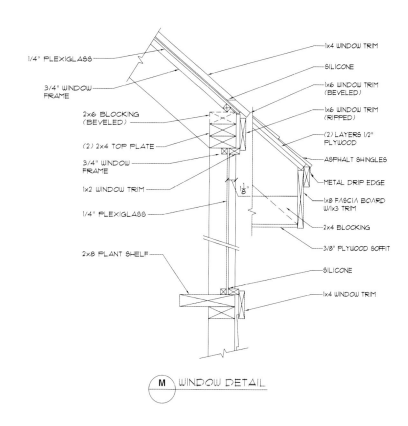

M WINDOW DETAIL

21. Insert plexiglass for the windows at the front and right wall. Run a bead of silicone around the perimeter of the glass before fastening 1x2 window trim with 6d galvanized nails. Apply a bead of silicone at the corners where the plexiglass and trim meet.

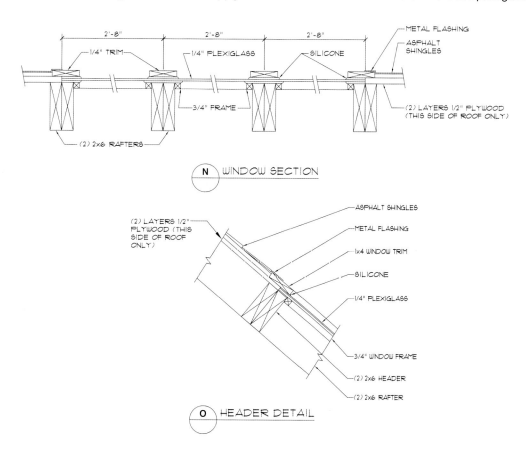

N WINDOW SECTION

O HEADER DETAIL

FINISHED ROOFING

22. Apply a second layer of 1/2" plywood to the right side of the roof making the roof surface flush with the 1x4 window trim.

23. Apply metal flashing to the 1x4 trim around the window using silicone and 8d galvanized nails as shown in details N and O.

24. Apply 1x8 fascia board and 1x3 trim board with 8d galvanized nails.

25. Apply the 15# roofing felt with 7/8" roofing nails. Start at the bottom of the roof and overlap the felt 4".

26. Cut (13) 2x4 blocks 11 1/2" long for the overhangs. See details M and P. Nail the blocks at each rafter location. Apply 3/8" plywood to the underside of overhangs with 6d galvanized nails.

27. Apply the roof shingles per manufacturer's instructions. Run a bead of silicone around the window where the shingles meet the 1x4 trim.

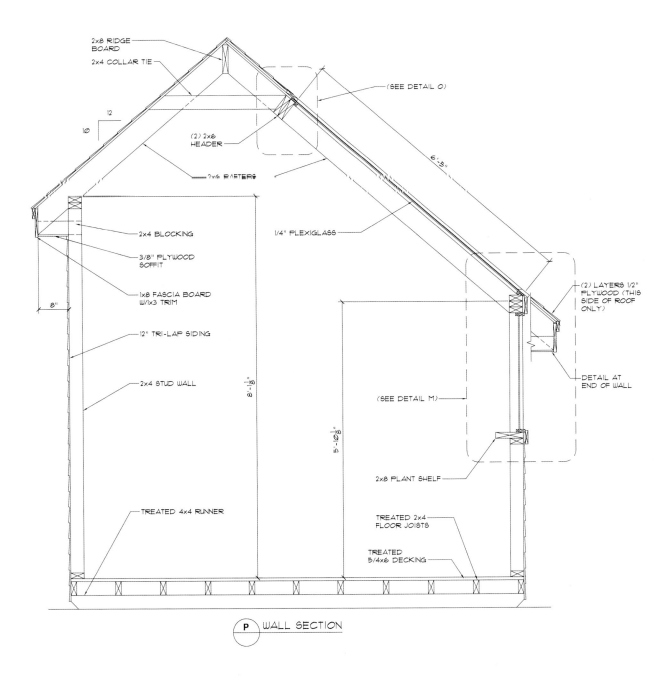

P WALL SECTION

SIDING

28. Cut 12" tri-lap hardboard siding to size for each wall as indicated in the wall elevations as shown below, detail S. Start the first row 2" up from the bottom of the 4x4 runners, making sure the siding is level. Fasten the siding with (2) 8d galvanized siding nails at every stud.

WOOD VENTS DOOR AND RAMP

29. Install wood vents per manufacturer's instructions. Cut 1x4 trim and fasten with 8d galvanized nails.

30. Install 3'-0"x6'-8" door per manufacturer's instructions. Cut 1x4 door trim and fasten with 8d galvanized nails. Install 4 1/2"x36" metal drip edge at door sill.

31. Cut treated 2x6 boards for the frame and 2x6 decking as shown detail Q. Screw the ramp together with 3" galvanized screws.

FINISH AND TRIM

32. Cut 1x4 corner boards as shown on elevations below. Fasten in place with 8d galvanized nails.

33. Paint and/or stain as desired per manufacturer's instructions.

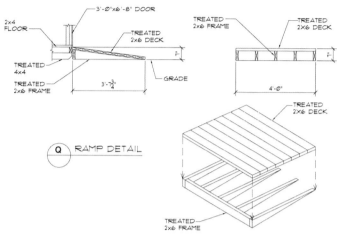

Q RAMP DETAIL

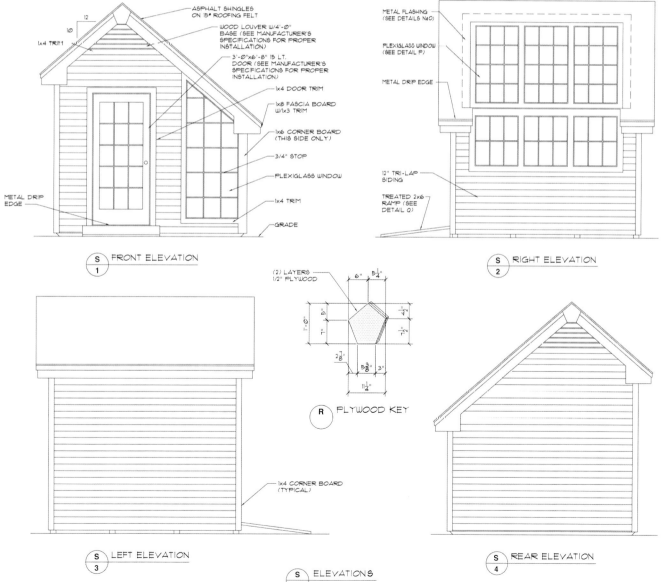

S FRONT ELEVATION 1

S RIGHT ELEVATION 2

R PLYWOOD KEY

S LEFT ELEVATION 3

S ELEVATIONS

S REAR ELEVATION 4

The Marianna

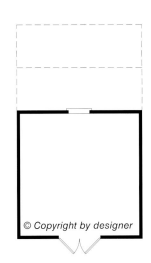

© Copyright by designer

The Marianna barn storage shed is a taller style shed that enjoys a classic barnyard look thanks to its Gambrel roof style. This shed looks great near a garden, or anywhere on your property especially in a rural setting, and it also includes handy loft storage above.

- Three popular sizes -
  12' x 12'   12' x 16'   12' x 20'
- Slab foundation
- Building height - 12'-10"
- Ceiling height - 7'-4"
- 4' x 6'-8" double-door for easy access
- Material list included
- Step-by-step instructions included

The Monessen

© Copyright by designer

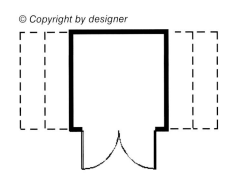

The Monessen Salt box style storage shed offers complete flexibility since it can be built to be as big as 16' x 8', or as small as 8' x 8'. Whatever works best for your needs and your lot size. Total flexibility is a great feature with this stylish shed!

- Three popular sizes -
  8' x 8'   12' x 8'   16' x 8'
- Concrete slab or wood deck on gravel foundation
- Building height - 8'-2"
- Front wall height - 7'
- 6' x 6'-5" double-door for easy access
- Material list included
- Step-by-step instructions included

PLAN #F55-002D-4506

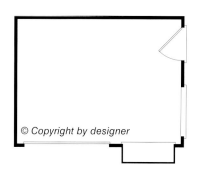

© Copyright by designer

- Size - 16' x 12'
- 192 square feet
- Slab foundation
- Building height - 12'-4 1/2"
- Ceiling height - 8'
- 8' x 7' overhead door
- Material list included
- Step-by-step instructions included

PLAN #F55-002D-4515

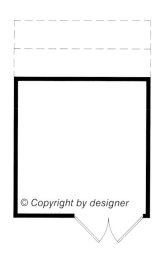

© Copyright by designer

- Three popular sizes -
  10' x 10'   12' x 10'   14' x 10'
- Wood floor on 4x6 runners foundation
- Building height - 10'-11"
- Rear wall height - 7'-3"
- 5' x 6'-9" double-door for easy access
- Material list included
- Step-by-step instructions included

The Maddy

The Maddy convenience shed is the perfect all-purpose shed design that features a garage door style entry as well as another side entry door. Two windows brighten the interior superbly and it would also be ideal for lawn equipment or small boat storage.

The Maxine

The Maxine expandable garden shed is an attractive shed that has clerestory windows for added light. With an interior rear wall height of 7'-3", and a 5' x 6'-9" double-door, this shed is easy-to-access.

The Maude

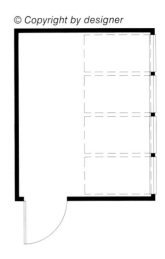

© Copyright by designer

The Maude garden shed has large skylight windows for optimal plant growth and ample room for tool and lawn equipment storage. Start enjoying your own organic veggies year-round with help from this handy shed!

- Size - 10' x 12'
- 120 square feet
- Wood floor on gravel base foundation
- Building height - 9'-9"
- Rear wall height - 7'-1 1/2"
- Material list included
- Step-by-step instructions included

The Henwood

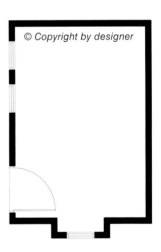

© Copyright by designer

The Henwood is a shed with tons of charm and would go perfectly residing in the backyard alongside a Modern Farmhouse style home. The windows and door allow for ample sunlight. This shed would be great used for storage, or even a backyard office. There are so many great uses available for the attractive Henwood shed!

- Size - 10' x 15'
- 144 square feet
- Slab foundation
- Building height - 15'
- Ceiling height - 9'

PLAN #F55-002D-4520

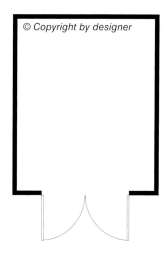

© Copyright by designer

- Size - 10' x 12'
- 120 square feet
- Wood floor on 4x4 runners foundation
- Building height - 10'-7"
- Ceiling height - 6'-11"
- 6' x 6'-2" double-door for easy access
- Material list included
- Step-by-step instructions included

PLAN #F55-002D-4521

© Copyright by designer

- Size - 12' x 16'
- 192 square feet
- Slab foundation
- Building height - 12'-5"
- Ceiling height - 8'
- 8' x 7' overhead door for easy entry
- Material list included
- Step-by-step instructions included

The Rasmussen

The Rasmussen yard barn with loft storage is a charming barn style shed that matches true country style without a hitch. Double front doors and a Gambrel style roof create an easy-to-use interior space, while the loft door provides additional storage space above.

The Marcella

The Marcella barn storage shed has an 8' x 7' overhead garage style door that makes entry easy especially with large equipment or your tractor. A window adds light to the interior offering ease when trying to locate items inside.

The Penney

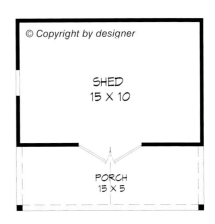

© Copyright by designer

SHED
15 X 10

PORCH
15 X 5

The Penney is the perfect rustic Craftsman shed offering a double-door entry to the inside for ease with larger items and a covered front porch making it also a nice place to relax, or store firewood in a dry, sheltered place.

- Size - 15' x 15'
- 225 total square feet -
  Shed - 150
  Porch - 75
- Wood floor joists over treated girders foundation
- Building height - 14'
- Ceiling height - 8'

The Marilyn

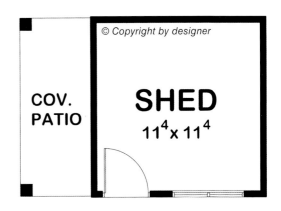

© Copyright by designer

COV.
PATIO

SHED
11^4 x 11^4

The Marilyn shed is an attractive shed that complements any style of home. It has covered storage and a friendly double-window brightening the interior. Designed to appear like a cottage, the convenient wide roof overhang is perfect for keeping items safe from the elements.

- Size - 17' x 12'
- 204 total square feet
  Shed - 144
  Covered patio - 60
- Slab foundation
- Building height - 16'-10"
- Ceiling height - 9'

PLAN #F55-127D-4514

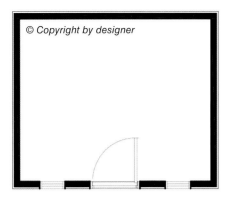

© Copyright by designer

- 9 sizes available -
12' x 8'	14' x 8'	16' x 8'
12' x 10'	14' x 10'	16' x 10'
12' x 12'	14' x 12'	16' x 12'
- Wood floor on concrete blocks foundation
- Building heights -
  11'-4 1/2" with 8' depth
  11'-10 1/2" with 10' depth
  12'-4 1/2" with 12' depth
- Ceiling height - 7'-6"
- Construction prints are 8 1/2" x 11" in size

The expandable sleek and modern style of the Domani shed makes additional storage far from an eyesore. Built-in windows add natural light making it easy to locate its contents and the style is a great backyard focal point that far from detracts from your backyard aesthetic.

PLAN #F55-160D-4500

The Korbin

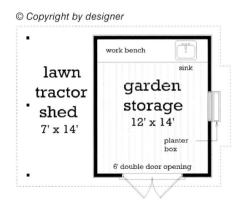

© Copyright by designer

lawn tractor shed 7' x 14'

work bench

sink

garden storage 12' x 14'

planter box

6' double door opening

- Size - 19' x 14'
- 266 total square feet -
  Garden storage - 168
  Lawn tractor shed - 98
- Raised wood floor or slab foundation, please specify when ordering
- Building height - 16'

The Korbin barn shed offers great country style in addition to being a handy yard accessory. The covered side porch creates dry storage for firewood, a tractor, or other items guarding them from the elements. A planter box window adds curb appeal and the work bench and sink inside make gardening a breeze.

The Jennar

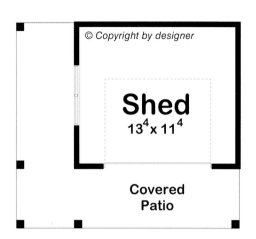

The Jennar shed has a wrap-around porch with a wide double-door that opens overhead. Its wrap-around covered porch design is perfect for firewood storage or even a little outdoor escape. The decorative dormer adds light to the interior and great style on the exterior.

- Size - 19' x 17'
- 323 total square feet
  Shed - 168
  Covered patio - 155
- Slab foundation
- Building height - 16'
- Ceiling height - 9'

The Colmar

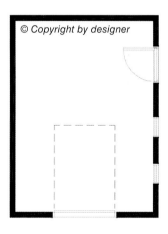

The Colmar practical garden shed offers a sleek exterior that would look terrific with today's popular Modern Farmhouse style home. Two windows, an entry door, and a side garage door make this stylish shed totally accessible in many areas!

- 9 sizes available -
12' x 10'	14' x 10'	16' x 10'
12' x 12'	14' x 12'	16' x 12'
12' x 14'	14' x 14'	16' x 14'
- Wood floor on concrete blocks foundation
- Building heights -
  12' with 15'-9", 14' with 16'-9", 16' with 17'-9"
- Ceiling height - 7'-6"
- Construction prints are 8 1/2" x 11" in size

PLAN #F55-125D-4504

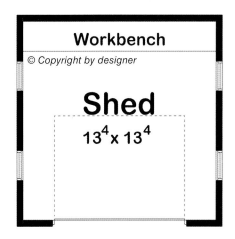

Workbench
© Copyright by designer
Shed
13⁴ x 13⁴

- Size - 14' x 14'
- 196 square feet
- Slab foundation
- Building height - 17'
- Ceiling height - 9'

PLAN #F55-165D-4502

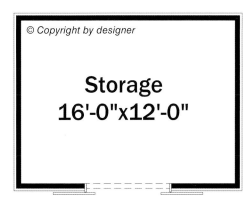

© Copyright by designer
Storage
16'-0"x12'-0"

- Size - 16' x 12'
- 192 square feet
- Slab foundation
- Building height - 12'-6"
- Ceiling height - 8'

The Abrantes

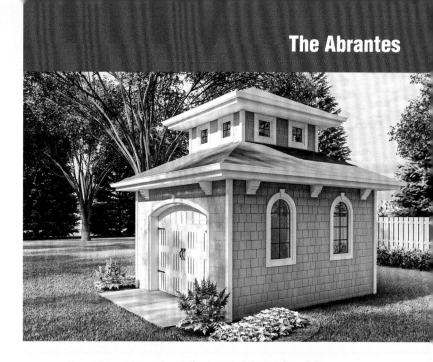

The Abrantes shed is a solid choice if you have a Craftsman or Modern Farmhouse style home since it allows you to keep the architectural style of your home and shed consistent. The unique roof clerestory window adds plentiful light and a handy work bench runs the entire width in the back.

The Novak

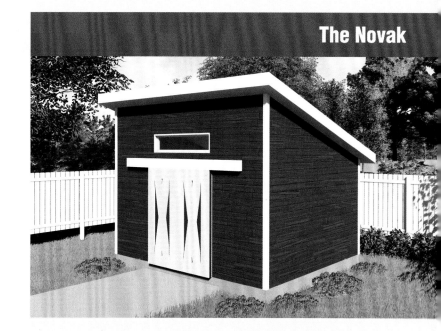

The Novak modern shed is an economical and easy-to-build modern-inspired shed that features a barn-style sliding door entry with a transom window above for added light to the interior. This is the stylish solution for your backyard storage needs!

The Hagge

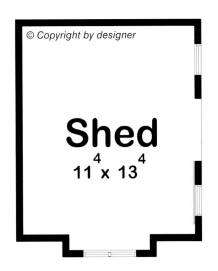

© Copyright by designer

Shed
11'-4" x 13'-4"

The Hagge storage shed is a functional design with a stylish box bay window on one end. This is a great shed to build alongside a patio, pool, or even a fire pit area. Store all of your backyard essentials for every season in style!

- Size - 12' x 15'
- 174 total square feet
- Slab foundation
- Building height - 15'
- Ceiling height - 9'

The Weslan

© Copyright by designer

STORAGE 7 X 9

BATH 7 X 9

SHWR 4 X 4

WORKSHOP 14 X 20

For those of you who can't tear away from your favorite hobbies and home projects, the Weslan workshop includes a full bath and plenty of space for those late nights when you decide to crash on the couch and finish the project in the wee hours the next morning.

- Size - 15' x 30'
- 450 total square feet -
  Workshop - 383
  Bath - 67
- Slab foundation standard; pier/girder available for an additional fee
- 1 full bath
- Building height - 13'-6"
- Ceiling height - 9'

PLAN #F55-113D-4514

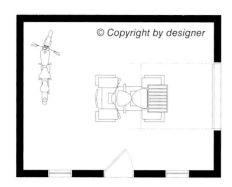

© Copyright by designer

- Size - 20' x 15'-5"
- 309 square feet
- Monolithic slab foundation
- Building height - 15'-10"
- Ceiling height - 8'
- 2" x 6" exterior walls

The Richman

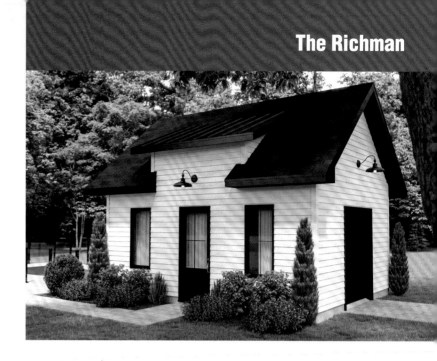

The Richman Modern Farmhouse style storage shed is a nice, modest sized storage shed that is designed with today's favorite home styles in mind. It's the perfect shed for keeping yard equipment out of sight and stored in the most stylish way.

PLAN #F55-002D-4502

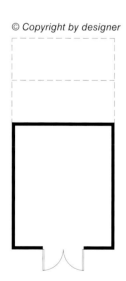

© Copyright by designer

- Three popular sizes -
  10' x 12'   10' x 16'   10' x 20'
- Wood floor on 4x4 runners foundation
- Building height - 8'-4 1/2"
- Ceiling height - 6'-4"
- 4' x 6'-4" double-door for easy access
- Material list included
- Step-by-step instructions included

The Carmen Cove

The expandable Carmen Cove yard barn is available in three popular sizes. This mini-sized barn provides an ample storage solution for your lawn or garden equipment and it includes a 4' x 6'-4" double-door for easy access.

The Blondell

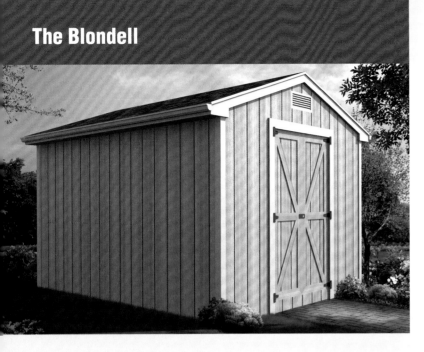

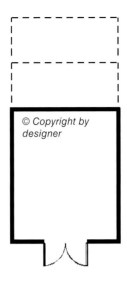

The Blondell shed has that perfect classic shed style that looks great in any backyard setting. Use it to store yard equipment, patio furniture in the off-season, or gardening supplies. An oversized double door entry makes removing items a cinch.

- Three popular sizes -
  10' x 12'   10' x 16'   10' x 20'
- Wood floor on 4x4 runners foundation
- Building height - 8'-8 1/2"
- Ceiling height - 7'
- 4' x 6'-4" double-door for easy access
- Material list included
- Step-by-step instructions included

The Sherry Hill

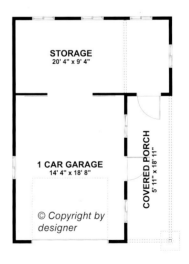

STORAGE
20' 4" x 9' 4"

1 CAR GARAGE
14' 4" x 18' 8"

© Copyright by designer

COVERED PORCH
5' 11" x 18' 11"

The Sherry Hill classic barn-style shed can also double as a one-car garage. It offers a large storage space on the main floor for convenience, and a covered side porch, ideal for just relaxing in the shade and watching the kid's play outdoors.

- Size - 21' x 29'
- 495 square feet
- Monolithic slab foundation
- Building height - 18'-6"
- Ceiling height - 10'

PLAN #F55-002D-4503

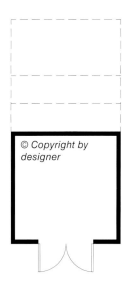

© Copyright by designer

- Four popular sizes -
  - 8' x 8'   8' x 12'
  - 8' x 10'   8' x 16'
- Wood floor on 4x4 runners
- Building height - 8'-4"
- Ceiling height - 6'-9"
- 4' x 6'-5" double-door for easy access
- Material list included
- Step-by-step instructions included

The Blair gable storage shed is an economical and expandable shed that can be built in four popular sizes. The oversized double door makes access easy for grabbing lawn equipment, patio furniture cushions, or even pet supplies.

PLAN #F55-125D-4510

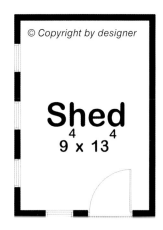

© Copyright by designer

Shed
9⁴ x 13⁴

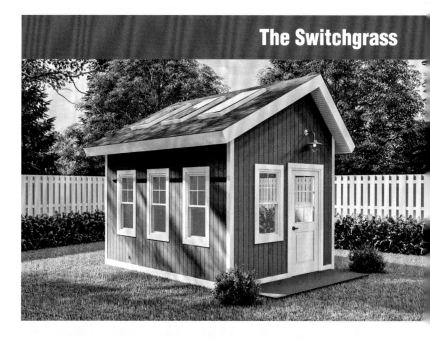

- Size - 10' x 14'
- 140 square feet
- Slab foundation
- Building height - 14'
- Ceiling height - 9'

The Switchgrass shed plan is glowing with natural light. Three skylight windows occupy the gable roof, while four more windows lie below. The Switchgrass is the perfect backyard shed for any house style. Look no further if you've been searching for a sunny shed!

The Shaw

© Copyright by designer

Storage
30'-0"x14'-0"

The Shaw sleek Modern Farmhouse shed looks fantastic with any style of home, but especially with today's Modern Farmhouse style. It's the perfect spot for potting plants since it includes Double French sliding doors and multiple windows illuminating the interior perfectly for any task at hand.

- Size - 30' x 14'
- 420 square feet
- Slab foundation
- Building height - 12'-8"
- Ceiling height - 8'

The Wyman

STOOP

LAWN EQUIP.
15 x 8

STOR
4 x 8

VAULTED
SHOP
19 x 11

© Copyright by designer

STOOP

The Wyman vaulted shop is ideal for do-it-yourselfers who like to partake in a variety of tasks. The spacious shop has a double door flanked by windows for added light and a storage closet. On the outside is a separate lawn equipment storage area accessible by another double door.

- Size - 20' x 20'
- 400 square feet
- Slab foundation
- Building height - 14'-7"
- Ceiling height - 8'

PLAN #F55-002D-4508

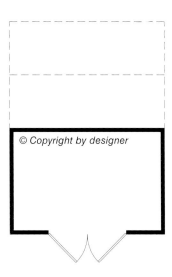

© Copyright by designer

- Three popular sizes -
  12' x 8'   12' x 12'   12' x 16'
- Concrete slab or wood deck on block piers foundation
- Building height - 9'-10"
- Ceiling height - 7'-10"
- 5'-6" x 6'-8" double-door for easy access
- Material list included
- Step-by-step instructions included

PLAN #F55-002D-4524

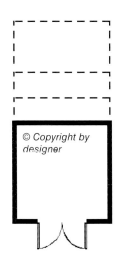

© Copyright by designer

- Four popular sizes -
  8' x 8'   8' x 12'
  8' x 10'   8' x 16'
- Wood floor on 4x4 runners foundation
- Building height - 7'-6"
- Ceiling height - 6'
- 4' x 6' double-door for easy access
- Material list included
- Step-by-step instructions included

The Marcia

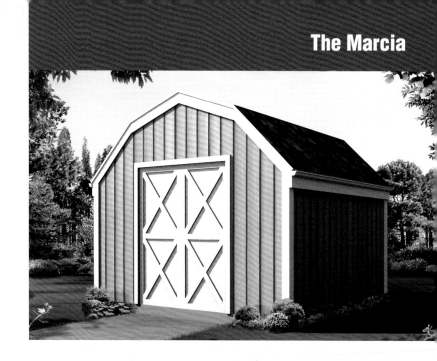

The Gambrel style roof design of the expandable Marcia storage shed gives it a pleasing country style. This shed allows easy access thanks to its 5'-6" x 6'-8" double-door entry and it can easily be built in three popular sizes.

The Norris

The Norris is an attractive style expandable shed that can be built in four popular sizes and is perfect for the storage of lawn and garden equipment, or other household necessities. This shed also has a 4' x 6' double-door for easy access.

The Terry

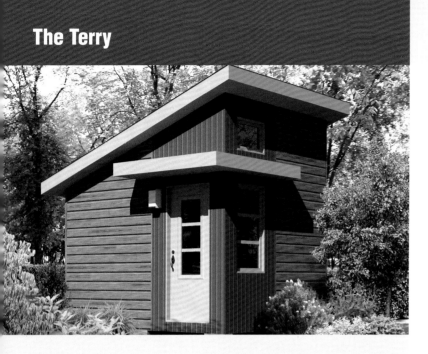

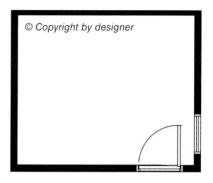

© Copyright by designer

The Terry modern style shed will quickly become one of your favorite things about your backyard. From its slant roof design to its mixed use of horizontal and vertical siding, this shed is loaded with personality and unbeatable style that everyone is sure to comment about.

- 15 sizes available -

8' x 8'	8' x 10'	8' x 12'
10' x 8'	12' x 8'	14' x 8'
16' x 8'	10' x 10'	12' x 10'
12' x 12'	14' x 12'	14' x 10'
14' x 12'	16' x 10'	16' x 12'

- Wood floor on concrete blocks foundation
- Ceiling height - 7'-6" vaulted
- Construction prints are 8 1/2" x 11"

The Brinley

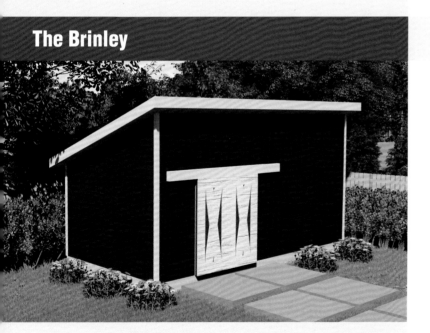

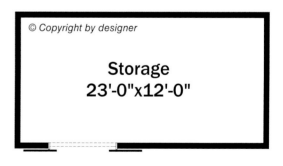

© Copyright by designer

Storage
23'-0"x12'-0"

The Brinley modern garden shed provides the perfect amount of space for lawn necessities, gardening supplies, or seasonal yard decor. No need to store everything in the basement and deal with the hassle of getting ready for spring, this shed is convenient and waiting for you in your own backyard!

- Size - 23' x 12'
- 176 square feet
- Slab foundation
- Building height - 12'-6"
- Ceiling height - 8'

PLAN #F55-142D-4507

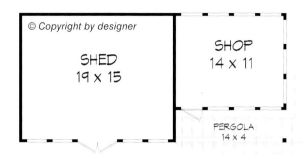

- Size - 34' x 16'
- 488 total square feet
  - Shed - 285
  - Shop - 154
  - Pergola - 49
- Slab foundation
- Building height - 17'-7"
- Ceiling height - 9'

PLAN #F55-165D-4501

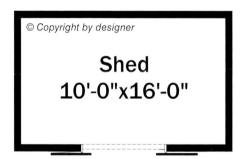

- Size - 16' x 10'
- 160 square feet
- Slab foundation
- Building height - 12'-3"
- Ceiling height - 8'

The Fuller

The Fuller shed has tons of personality and will make you smile when you lay your eyes on it. Enter double-doors and find a sizable space for overflow items. To the right is a sun-filled shop with a separate door and outdoor pergola above. It will be easy to stay all day in this pleasant sun-filled space.

The Boxwood

The Boxwood barn door shed is a simple, functional and versatile shed ideal for providing stylish storage right in your own backyard. Popular barn style sliding doors make yard equipment and gardening supplies super easy to access, while providing a stylish, universally pleasing exterior.

The Marjorie

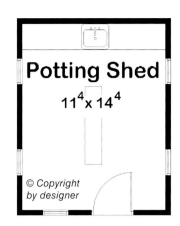

Potting Shed

11⁴ x 14⁴

© Copyright
by designer

The Marjorie potting shed with sink and a built-in counter top is a lovely shed ideal for the gardening enthusiast. Multiple windows illuminate the space providing the perfect tranquil and cheerful spot for potting plants, or tending to your herb garden.

- Size - 12' x 15'
- 180 square feet
- Slab foundation
- Building height - 14'-4"
- Ceiling height - 9'

The Martha

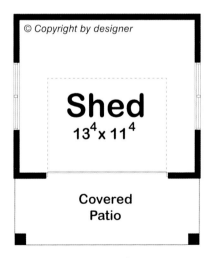

© Copyright by designer

Shed

13⁴ x 11⁴

Covered
Patio

The Martha shed with covered porch could also double as a garage if a standard one-car garage sized roll-up door is used. Large double-hung windows on each side offer plenty of natural light inside and the cottage-like exterior greatly adds to its curb appeal.

- Size - 14' x 17'
- 238 total square feet
  Shed - 168
  Covered patio - 70
- Slab foundation
- Building height - 16'
- Ceiling height - 9'

PLAN #F55-002D-4510

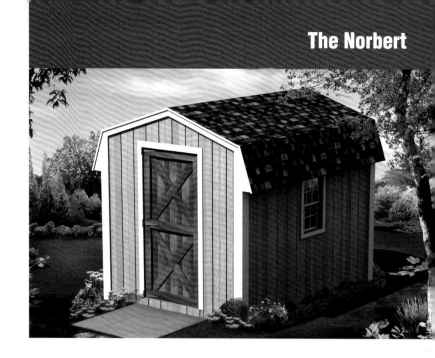

- Four popular sizes -
  - 7'-3" x 6'   7'-3" x 10'
  - 7'-3" x 8'   7'-3" x 12'
- Wood floor on 4x4 runners or concrete slab foundation
- Building height - 9'
- Ceiling height - 7'-4"
- Material list included
- Step-by-step instructions included

The Norbert expandable mini barn storage shed includes four popular sizes allowing you to find the perfect fit for any size lot. With its attractive gambrel style roof, it has a classic barn feel that looks nice with country style homes and locales.

PLAN #F55-125D-4511

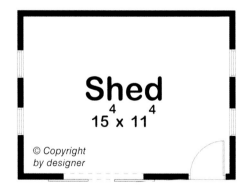

Shed
15 x 11

© Copyright by designer

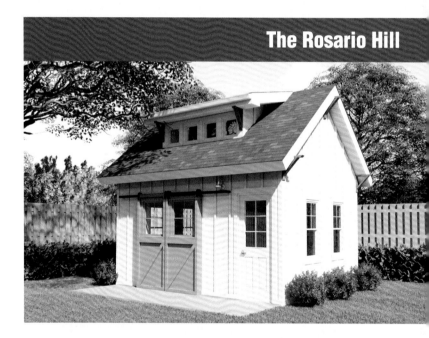

- Size - 16' x 12'
- 192 square feet
- Slab foundation
- Building height - 15'
- Ceiling height - 9'

The Rosario Hill shed is a pleasant design homeowners today will just love. The shed dormer on the roof adds plenty of extra sunlight to the interior and tons of curb appeal. Thanks to its attractive style, it could easily be converted to a children's playhouse if extra storage is no longer needed.

The Gates

The Gates modern garden shed has a unique angled shape with a center door flanked by transoms on two walls for plenty of sunlight. Choose a modern style door design and add the ability for even more sunlight. This shed is bound to create quite a "buzz" in your backyard garden.

PLAN #F55-127D-4515

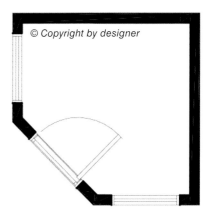

- Four popular sizes -
  - 8' x 8'   12' x 12'
  - 10' x 10'   14' x 14'
- Wood floor on concrete blocks foundation
- Building heights -
  - 12' with 8' depth
  - 12'-6" with 10' depth
  - 13' with 12' depth
  - 13'-6" with 14' depth
- Front wall height - 7'-6"
- Construction prints are 8 1/2" x 11" in size

The George

The George innovative shed has a stylish exterior that looks great with rustic and Craftsman style homes. The slant roof line allows for a sunny transom above the door and adequate head space when entering to locate items inside.

PLAN #F55-127D-4513

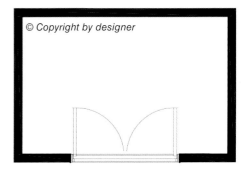

- 15 sizes available -

8' x 8'	8' x 10'	8' x 12'
10' x 8'	12' x 8'	14' x 8'
16' x 8'	10' x 10'	12' x 10'
12' x 12'	14' x 12'	14' x 10'
14' x 12'	16' x 10'	16' x 12'

- Wood floor on concrete blocks foundation
- Building heights - 12'-1" with 8' width, 12'-9" with 10' width 13'-5" with 12' width
- Ceiling heights - 7'-6" vaults to 10'-2" with 8' depth, 10'-10" with 10' depth, 11'-6" with 12' depth
- Construction prints are 8 1/2" x 11" in size

Larger Shed Plans

Plan #F55-136D-7501 on page 85

Larger shed plans provide an attractive way to house all of those extras homeowners need. These do-it-yourself building plans include larger structures such as barns, pole buildings, and workshops among other innovative designs. These building plans are easy-to-follow making it easy to add a larger shed to your lot or property. Make life easier and build one of these functional structures for your yard, farm or land.

The McDonald Pole Building Plan

The McDonald pole build building equipment shed is a functional and versatile structure that can easily be lengthened by adding 10' bays on the right side. The separate shop area with door creates the perfect workshop scenario for farm supplies, a mechanic shop space, or even a more sheltered storage space away from the elements for other do-it-yourself projects that can be done year-round. This pole building shed is ideal for those passionate about projects, or the car enthusiast!

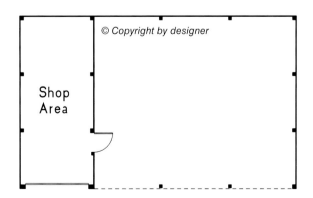

© Copyright by designer

Shop Area

PLAN #F55-002D-7505

- Size - 40' x 24'
- 960 square feet
- Floating slab foundation
- Building height - 14'-4"
- Ceiling height - 10'
- 9' x 8' overhead door
- Material list included
- Step-by-step instructions included

QTY.	SIZE	DESCRIPTION
6 pcs.	6x6x18'	Treated posts
10 pcs.	6x6x14'	Treated posts
1 pc.	4x4x14'	Treated posts
8 pcs.	2x6x20'	Treated skirt boards
18 pcs.	2x6x16'	Treated skirt boards
1 pcs.	2x6x8'	Treated skirt boards
8 pcs.	2x12x20'	Girder-rafter supports
3 pcs.	2x12x16'	Girder-rafter supports
4 pcs.	2x6x20'	Intermediate girts
9 pcs.	2x6x16'	Intermediate girts
6 pcs.	2x4x8'	Diagonal kneebrace
8 pcs.	2x4x16'	Diagonal wind brace and blocking
2 pcs.	2x6x10'	Garage door blocking
3 pcs.	2x8x10'	Garage door jambs
3 pcs.	2x6x10'	Garage hardware casing
3 pcs.	2x6x12'	Truss tie down blocks
5 pcs.	2x4x16'	Truss lateral bracing
6 pcs.	2x4x18'	Diagonal truss bracing
3 pcs.	2x4x10'	Garage door hardware casing
15		"W" roof trusses 24'-0" span
2		Gable end roof trusses 24'-0" span
640 l.f.	2x4	Roof purlin
80 l.f.	1x8	Fascia
3 pcs.	2x8x10'	Door jambs
2 pcs.	2x8x10'	Door header
1	9'-0"x8'-0"	Sectional up and over garage door complete with all necessary hardware
1	2'-8"x6'-8"x1 3/8"	Garage service door 5 panel
1 pair	3 1/2"x3 1/2"	Door butts
1		Key in knob cylinder lockset
44 l.f.	1x4	Garage door stop
2 1/2 cu. yds.		Concrete for post footings
3 cu. yds.		Concrete for floor in shop area (concrete figures based upon level site conditions)
34 pcs.	50.3"x8'-0"	Galvanized or aluminum ribbed siding panels 48" exposed
40 pcs.	50.3"x8'-0"	Galvanized or aluminum ribbed roofing panels 48" exposed
40 l.f.		Vented gable roof edge
100 l.f.		Galvanized or aluminum rake edge member
80 l.f.		Eave flashing

MATERIAL FOR ONE 10'-0" INTERMEDIATE BAY UNIT

QTY.	SIZE	DESCRIPTION
2 pcs.	6x6x14'	Treated post
2 pcs.	2x6x20'	Treated skirt boards
4 pcs.	2x12x10'	Grits rafter support
2 pcs.	2x6x10'	Intermediate girts
2 pcs.	2x4x8'	Lateral brace
2 pcs.	2x4x16'	Diagonal wind brace and blocking
1 pc.	2x6x12'	Truss tie down blocks
2 pcs.	2x4x12'	Truss lateral bracing
4		"W" roof trusses 24'-0" span
140 l.f.	2x4	Roof purlin
20 l.f.	1x8	Fascia
13 pcs.	50.3"x8'-0"	Galvanized or aluminum ribbed siding and roofing panels 48" exposed
1/24 cu. yd.		Concrete for post footings

NAILS FOR 24'x40' BUILDING

QTY.	SIZE	DESCRIPTION
4 lbs.	40d	Common nails coated
7 lbs.	20d	Common nails coated
12 lbs.	16d	Common nails coated
3 lbs.	12d	Common nails coated
4 lbs.	8d	Common nails coated
16 lbs.	2 1/4"	Screw shank nail with neoprene washer

LAYOUT AND EXCAVATION

1. Study the plan thoroughly. Be sure to check your local code requirements and if required obtain a building permit.

2. Stake outside perimeter of building with batter boards and place at least 2 or 3 feet back from each corner. Stretch string line to show complete perimeter to outside face of wall girts.

3. Remove sod, fill, compact and grade with bulldozer or tractor scoop. The amount of site preparation depends on the use of the building. Little site preparation may be needed for a storage structure except to keep runoff water away. A livestock barn or other building used with concrete floors requires good drainage and a good base for a concrete floor.

4. Mark pole locations with small stakes. Remove stretched string lines.

5. Dig or bore pole holes using a power auger or backhoe 4' to 5' minimum deep and a minimum 16" to 24" diameter. Dig holes wide and deep enough to install pad or casing, if required.

6. Remove water or loose material from bottom of holes.

7. Place pad of concrete In bottom of hole, if required, and let cure for one day.

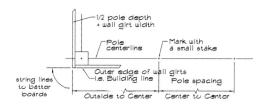

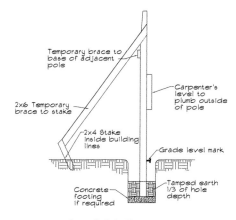

Figure 1. Location of poles or posts and string lines

SETTING THE POLES

8. Select 4 straight corner poles or timbers.

9. Place poles in holes. Let poles lean toward inside of building.

10. Replace string lines and plumb the two outside edges of the corner poles with a carpenter's level. Keep post 1 1/2" (width of girt) in from string line (see figure 1).

11. Drive 2x4 ground stakes within the building lines. Brace poles with 2x6 diagonals from ground stakes to upper portion of pole (see figures 2 and 3). Brace should be placed so that it will not interfere with the installation of the girder.

12. Locate, center and plumb outside edge of all intermediate poles. Brace with 2x6 ground stakes and 2x6 brace to adjacent poles. Double headed nails can be used to fasten bracing. Fill holes and tamp to approximately one third the depth. Note end bay or section is shorter than interior bays because dimensions are from outside of end wall girts to center of second pole (see figure 1).

13. Mark grade level with a nail driven partly into outer edge of each pole. Level can be set with engineer's level and rod.

Figure 2. Pole Alignment

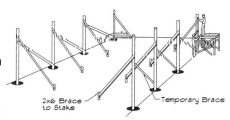

Figure 3. Temporary Bracing of Poles

INSTALLING GIRDERS

14. Measure and mark with a partly driven nail the bottom height of the 2x12 girders from the level grade mark. This height should be 9'-2 3/4" above the grade level mark. Cut a straight 2x4 to this dimension for fast and consistent marking from the grade level nails.

15. Nail a 2x4 girder support block on outside and inside of each pole with 6 or more 20d nails.

16. Cut 2x12 girders square and to exact length. Girders should butt at center line of poles except at corners. Check details on plan for lengths and nailing.

17. Build double girder with 2x6 truss tie down blocks about 18" long at the correct truss space (see figure 4). Start 40d nails near each end of double girder.

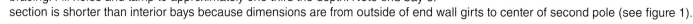
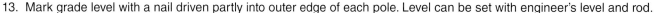

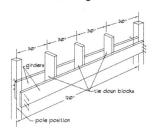

Figure 4 showing prebuilt girder with tie down blocks. Girder unit can be prebuilt on ground and installed as a complete unit.

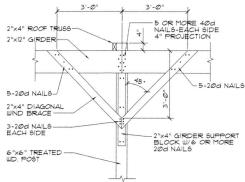

WIND BRACING & NAILING DETAIL

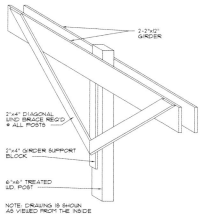

WIND BRACING DETAIL
ISOMETRIC

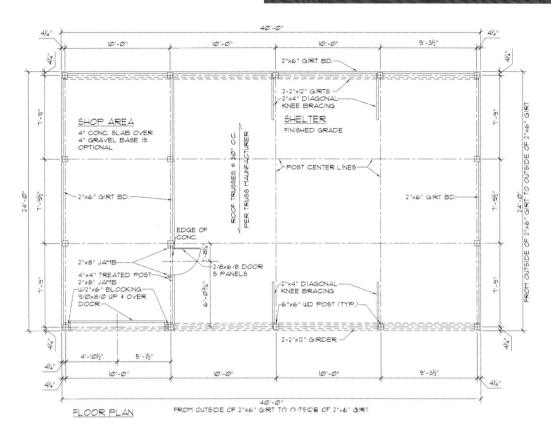

FLOOR PLAN — FROM OUTSIDE OF 2"x6" GIRT TO OUTSIDE OF 2"x6" GIRT

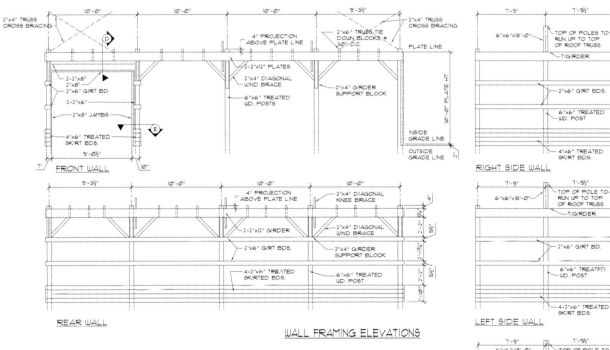

WALL FRAMING ELEVATIONS

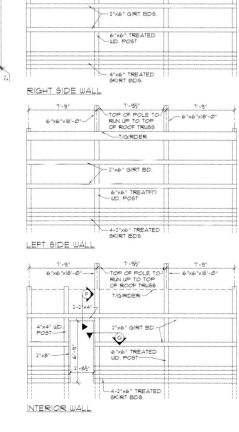

18. Place double girder on girder support blocks and nail at pole center line. Use truck bed or moving scaffold instead of ladders.

19. Check alignment of poles and girders. Move temporary braces or lateral supports if realignment is needed.

20. Install diagonal wind brace and complete girder nailing.

21. Remove string line. Fill and tamp all holes.

ROOF FRAMING

22. With the use of a crane place trusses on girders next to the poles and tie down blocking. Fasten trusses to poles and tie down blocking. Add 2x4 nailing strips and 2x4 knee bracing at each pole as shown on plan. See typical wall section.

23. Fasten several roof purlins 24" on center. Use spacers to check spacing. Roof purlins are butted over trusses. At ridge space purlins for vented gable ridge cap. Nail truss lateral bracing to lower chord of trusses.

24. Install roofing starting at lower corner so side laps are away from strongest winds. Corrugated sheets should be lapped one and one half corrugations. Lap ends 6" to 9". One nail per square foot is needed, use nails that do not corrode the roofing. Nail through the tops of the corrugations. Nails should penetrate at least 1" into the purlin.

25. Remove temporary pole bracing and use for wall girts. Install 4 pieces of 2x6 treated skirt boards as shown on elevation. Nail 2x6 girts on side and end walls as indicated on plans.

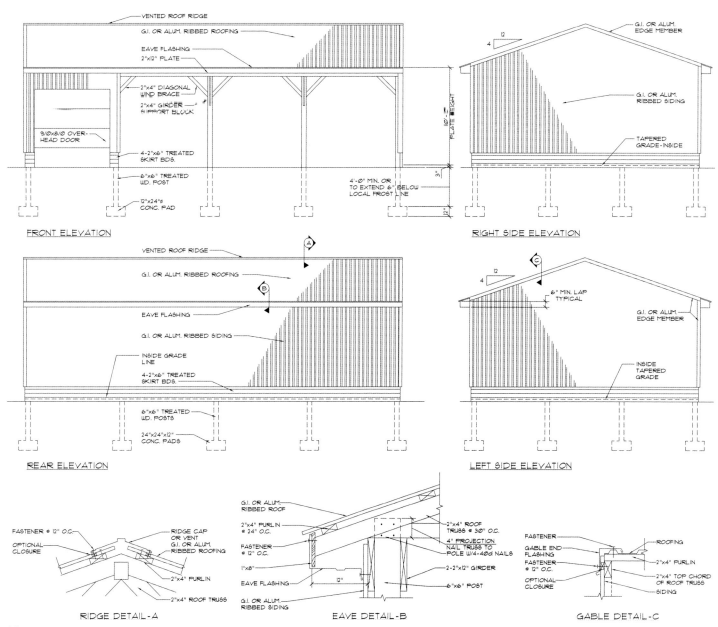

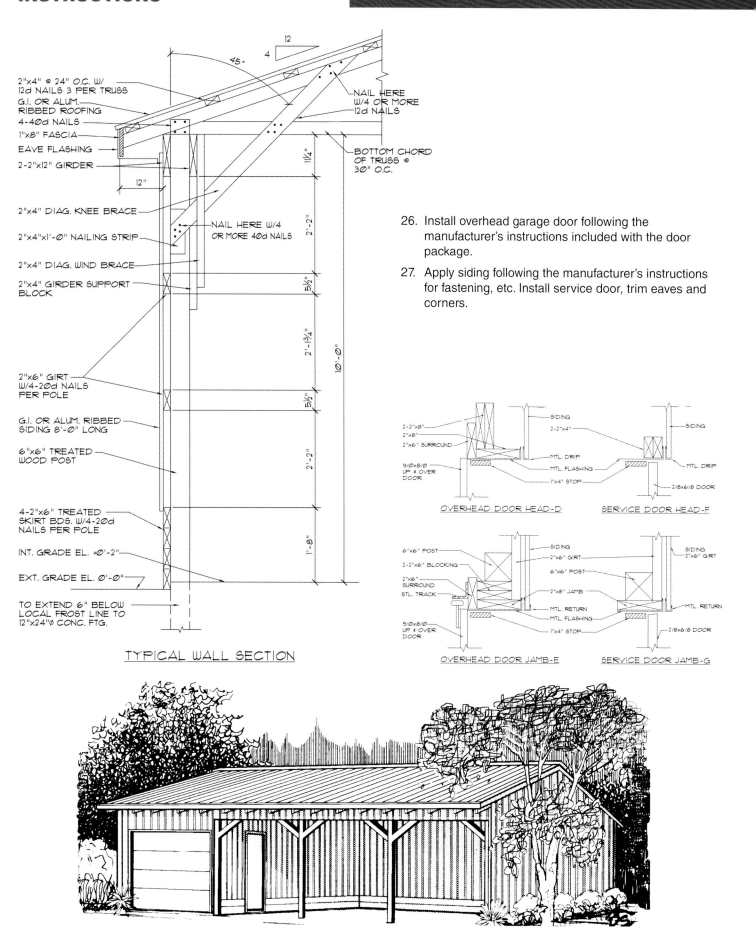

2"x4" @ 24" O.C. W/
12d NAILS 3 PER TRUSS
G.I. OR ALUM.
RIBBED ROOFING
4-40d NAILS
1"x8" FASCIA
EAVE FLASHING
2-2"x12" GIRDER

NAIL HERE
W/4 OR MORE
12d NAILS

BOTTOM CHORD
OF TRUSS @
30" O.C.

2"x4" DIAG. KNEE BRACE

NAIL HERE W/4
OR MORE 40d NAILS

2"x4"x1'-0" NAILING STRIP

2"x4" DIAG. WIND BRACE

2"x4" GIRDER SUPPORT
BLOCK

2"x6" GIRT
W/4-20d NAILS
PER POLE

G.I. OR ALUM. RIBBED
SIDING 8'-0" LONG

6"x6" TREATED
WOOD POST

4-2"x6" TREATED
SKIRT BDS. W/4-20d
NAILS PER POLE

INT. GRADE EL. +0'-2"

EXT. GRADE EL. 0'-0"

TO EXTEND 6" BELOW
LOCAL FROST LINE TO
12"x24"Ø CONC. FTG.

12

45°

12"

11¼"

2'-2"

5½"

2'-1¾"

10'-0"

5½"

2'-2"

1'-8"

TYPICAL WALL SECTION

26. Install overhead garage door following the manufacturer's instructions included with the door package.

27. Apply siding following the manufacturer's instructions for fastening, etc. Install service door, trim eaves and corners.

2-2"x8"
2"x8"
2"x6" SURROUND
9/0x8/0
UP & OVER
DOOR
SIDING
MTL. DRIP
MTL. FLASHING
1"x4" STOP

2-2"x4"
SIDING
MTL. DRIP
2/8x6/8 DOOR

OVERHEAD DOOR HEAD-D   **SERVICE DOOR HEAD-F**

6"x6" POST
2-2"x6" BLOCKING
2"x6" SURROUND
STL. TRACK
9/0x8/0
UP & OVER
DOOR
SIDING
2"x6" GIRT
6"x6" POST
2"x8" JAMB
MTL. RETURN
MTL. FLASHING
1"x4" STOP

SIDING
2"x6" GIRT
MTL. RETURN
2/8x6/8 DOOR

OVERHEAD DOOR JAMB-E   **SERVICE DOOR JAMB-G**

The Gilbert Mill

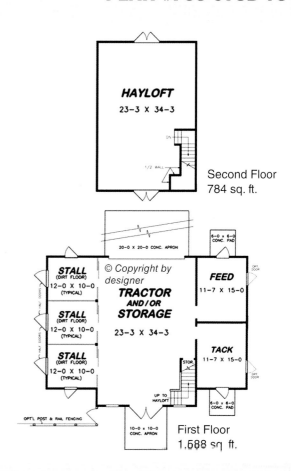

HAYLOFT
23-3 X 34-3

Second Floor
784 sq. ft.

STALL (DIRT FLOOR) 12-0 X 10-0 (TYPICAL)

STALL (DIRT FLOOR) 12-0 X 10-0 (TYPICAL)

STALL (DIRT FLOOR) 12-0 X 10-0 (TYPICAL)

© Copyright by designer

TRACTOR AND/OR STORAGE
23-3 X 34-3

20-0 X 20-0 CONC. APRON

FEED
11-7 X 15-0

TACK
11-7 X 15-0

6-0 X 6-0 CONC. PAD

6-0 X 6-0 CONC. PAD

STOR

UP TO HAYLOFT

OPT'L POST & RAIL FENCING

10-0 X 10-0 CONC. APRON

First Floor
1,588 sq. ft.

The Gilbert Mill barn is a great storage option with tractor storage, three horse stalls, tack and feed rooms, and a large second floor hayloft.

- Size - 48' x 35'
- 2,372 total square feet
  First floor - 1,588
  Second floor - 784
- Slab foundation
- Building height - 25'-6"
- Ceiling heights -
  First floor - 9'
  Second floor - 8'-4" to 28'

The Linfield

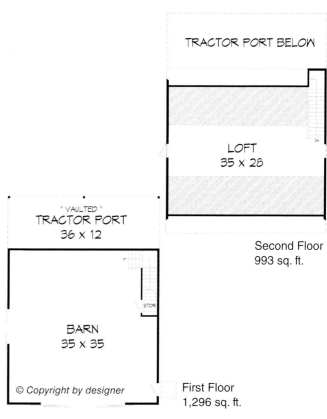

TRACTOR PORT BELOW

LOFT
35 x 28

Second Floor
993 sq. ft.

"VAULTED" TRACTOR PORT
36 x 12

STOR

BARN
35 x 35

© Copyright by designer

First Floor
1,296 sq. ft.

The Linfield barn has a vaulted covered tractor port on the exterior and a roomy second floor loft for hay and farming equipment.

- Size - 36' x 36'
- 2,289 total square feet
  First floor - 1,296
  Second floor - 993
- Slab foundation
- Building height - 29'-10"
- Ceiling heights -
  First floor - 10'
  Second floor - 10'
- 2" x 6" exterior walls

PLAN #F55-142D-7622

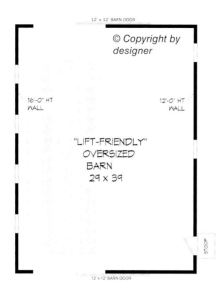

- Size - 30' x 40'
- 1,200 square feet
- Slab foundation
- Building height - 17'-8"
- Ceiling height - 12' vaults to 16'
- 2" x 6" exterior walls

The Waddell lift-friendly oversized barn has a modern style slant roof design and an easy-access barn style door that would look great with a Modern Farmhouse style home. Store extra home supplies, and vehicles such as an RV more easily and attractively.

PLAN #F55-136D-7501

The Betz Farm

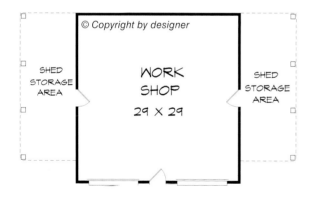

- Size - 50' x 30'
- 1,420 total square feet
  Workshop - 900
  Shed storage areas - 520
- Slab foundation
- Building height - 29'-9"
- Ceiling height - 12'

The Betz Farm storage barn and workshop has that classic "down on the farm" feel and features two front entry garage style doors leading to the workshop inside, and two side covered outdoor storage areas. Make this your special place for finishing all of the special projects on your list!

The Barclay

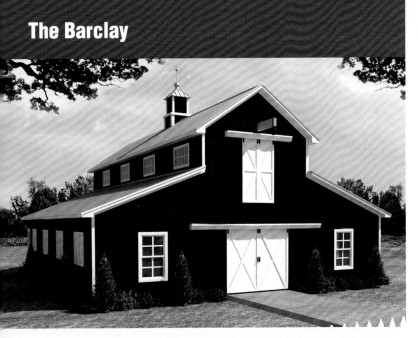

Second Floor
810 sq. ft.

© Copyright by designer

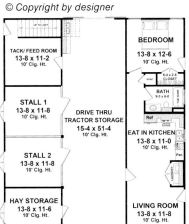

First Floor
2,289 sq. ft.

The Barclay barn offers total function for your farm or rural setting plus a one bedroom apartment with a full bath and kitchen.

- Size - 44' x 52'
- 3,099 total square feet
    Heated square feet - 741
    Unheated square feet - 2,358
- Slab foundation
- 1 bedroom, 1 full bath
- Building height - 26'-3"
- Ceiling heights -
    First floor - 10'
    Second floor - 9'

The Shemlock

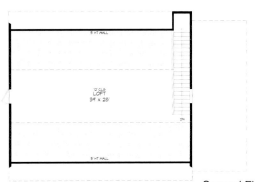

Second Floor
1,070 sq. ft.

© Copyright
by designer

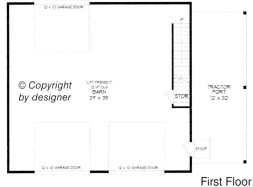

First Floor
1,440 sq. ft.

The Shemlock is the perfect size and style for those building a Farmhouse style home. The loft above adds tremendous extra space.

- Size - 52' x 36'
- 2,894 total square feet
    Barn - 1,440
    Loft - 1,070
    Tractor port - 384
- Slab foundation
- Building height - 31'-11"
- Ceiling heights -
    First floor - 12'
    Second floor - 12'

PLAN #F55-142D-7564

Second Floor
1,140 sq. ft.

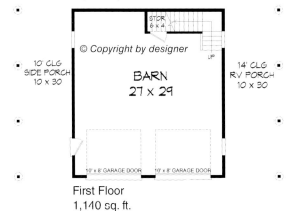

© Copyright by designer

First Floor
1,140 sq. ft.

PLAN #F55-142D-7530

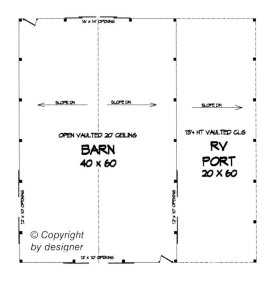

© Copyright by designer

- Size - 60' x 60'
- 3,600 total square feet
  Barn - 2,400
  RV Port - 1,200
- Post & beam foundation
- Building height - 30'-9"
- Ceiling heights -
  Barn - 20'
  RV Port - 13'+ vaulted

The Jennings Farm

The Jennings Farm barn has two floors with two garage doors, a full bath, two covered side porches and even more storage space above.

- Size - 48' x 30'
- 2,280 total square feet
  First floor - 1,140
  Second floor - 1,140
- Slab foundation
- 1 full bath
- Building height - 25'-9"
- Ceiling heights -
  First floor - 10'
  Second floor - 9'

The Sawmill Hill

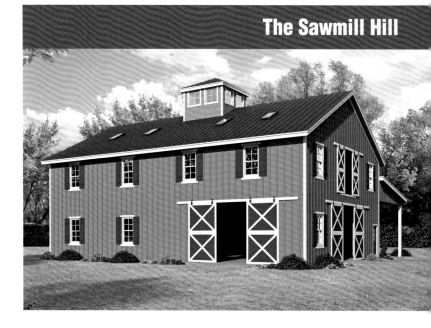

The Sawmill Hill barn has a soaring 20' vaulted ceiling with skylights above making this easily accessible without the need for electricity. Barn style doors on each side permit easy entry and a 15' height vaulted RV port will keep your recreational vehicle safe from the weather when not in use.

The Eiler Creek

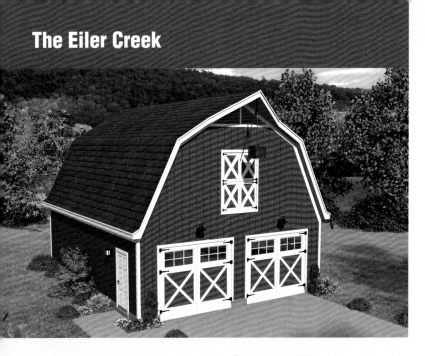

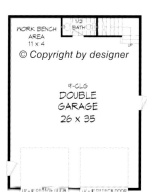

Second Floor
639 sq. ft.

LOFT
AREA
17 x 35
9'-CLG

WORK BENCH
AREA
11 x 4

1/2
BATH

DOUBLE
GARAGE
26 x 35
9'-CLG

© Copyright by designer

First Floor
1,008 sq. ft.

The Eiler Creek barn style garage has timeless farmstead style with two garage bays, a half bath, and a second floor loft area.

- Size - 28' x 36'
- 1,647 total square feet -
  First floor - 1,008
  Second floor - 639
- Slab foundation
- 1 half bath
- 2" x 6" exterior walls
- Building height - 25'-1"

The Mattox

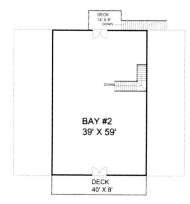

DECK
14' X 8'
DOWN

DOWN

BAY #2
39' X 59'

DECK
40' X 8'

Second Floor
2,400 sq. ft.

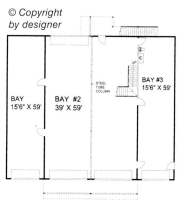

© Copyright
by designer

BAY
15'6" X 59'

BAY #2
39' X 59'

STEEL
TUBE
COLUMN

UP

BAY #3
15'6" X 59'

First Floor
4,320 sq. ft.

The Mattox two-level barn has four separate bays and a convenient half bath. Two staircases access the second floor inside and out.

- Size - 72' x 60'
- 6,720 square feet
- Slab foundation
- 1 half bath
- Ceiling heights -
  Bay #1 - 10'-8" vaults to 12'-10"
  Bay #2 - 14'-8"
  Bay #2, second floor - 12'-10"
  Bay #3 - 10'
- 2" x 6" exterior walls

PLAN #F55-125D-7508

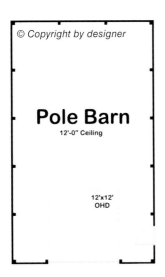

© Copyright by designer

Pole Barn
12'-0" Ceiling

12'x12'
OHD

- Size - 40' x 24'
- 960 square feet
- Slab foundation
- Post frame exterior walls
- Building height - 24'
- Ceiling height - 10'

The Washington Hill pole barn looks perfect with all country homes. Plenty of storage, a 12' x 12' overhead door and a side entry door make this a solid choice when it's time to select the perfect pole building for your property.

PLAN #F55-142D-7539

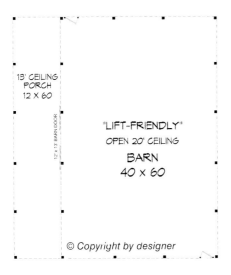

13' CEILING
PORCH
12 X 60

12' X 13' BARN DOOR

"LIFT-FRIENDLY"
OPEN 20' CEILING
BARN
40 x 60

© Copyright by designer

- Size - 40' x 60'
- 3,120 total square feet
  Barn - 2,400
  Covered porch - 720
- Slab foundation
- Building height - 38'-6"
- Ceiling heights -
  Barn - 20'
  Covered porch - 13'

The Crooked Barn is a lift-friendly oversized barn with a soaring 20' ceiling. The covered porch features a 13' tall ceiling, so storing large items is effortless. This is a handsome and functional addition to any rural setting.

The Newfield Creek

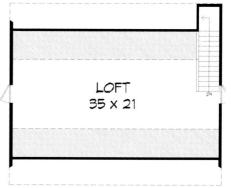

LOFT
35 x 21

Second Floor
777 sq. ft.

© Copyright
by designer

12' x 8' BARN DOOR

BARN
36 x 30

UP

STOR

20' x 8' BARN DOOR

First Floor
1,080 sq. ft.

The Newfield Creek barn with a loft is a stylish outbuilding option that provides additional space for farm equipment.

- Size - 36' x 30'
- 1,857 total square feet
  First floor - 1,080
  Second floor - 777
- Slab foundation
- Building height - 26'-6"
- Ceiling heights -
  First floor - 10'
  Second floor - 9'

The Harvest Run

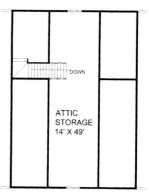

DOWN

ATTIC
STORAGE
14' X 49'

Second Floor
700 sq. ft.

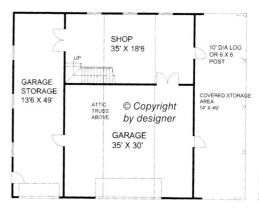

SHOP
35' X 18'6

10' DIA LOG
OR 6 X 6
POST

GARAGE
STORAGE
13'6 X 49'

UP

ATTIC
TRUSS
ABOVE

© Copyright
by designer

COVERED STORAGE
AREA
14' X 49'

GARAGE
35' X 30'

First Floor
2,500 sq. ft.

The Harvest Run combines a garage, shop and multiple storage places to create a high functioning two-level structure.

- Size - 64' x 50'
- 3,200 total square feet
  First floor - 2,500
  Second floor - 700
- Slab foundation
- Building height - 19'-9"
- Ceiling heights -
  First floor - 10'-8"
  Second floor - 7'
- 2" x 6" exterior walls

PLAN #F55-059D-6086

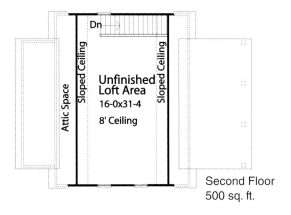

Second Floor
500 sq. ft.

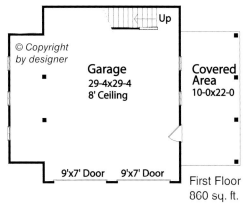

© Copyright by designer

First Floor
860 sq. ft.

PLAN #F55-002D-7511

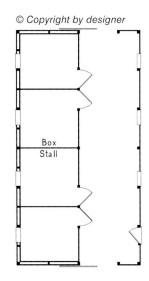

© Copyright by designer

Box Stall

- Size - 26' x 48'
- 1,248 square feet
- 6" x 6" poles in concrete casing foundation or concrete slab, please specify when ordering
- Building height - 22'
- Ceiling heights -
  First floor - 9'
  Loft - 11'
- Material list included
- Step-by-step instructions

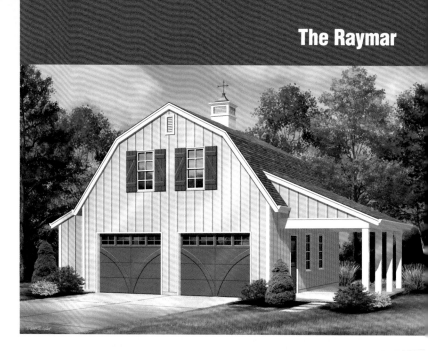

The Raymar

The Raymar is a 2-car garage/barn with classic farmstead style that offers space for two vehicles, a loft and a covered outdoor area.

- Size - 40'4" x 30'
- 1,360 total square feet
  First floor - 860
  Second floor - 500
- Footing and foundation wall foundation
- Building height - 21'-6"
- Ceiling heights -
  First floor - 8'
  Second floor - 8'

The Farmville

The Farmville horse barn features four box stalls on the main floor all with access to a larger storage area. There's also a loft above with even more room for hay or other equestrian essentials. Build the Farmville and complete your farm!

The Barnhill

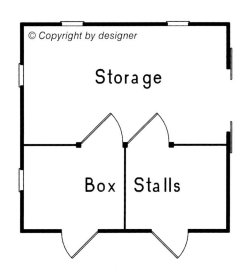

© Copyright by designer

The Barnhill is compact, yet has extra storage for feed, and two ample-sized box stalls with double doors for animals. The sliding side door into the storage area is 6' x 7' making it easy to access regardless of how large the item is to be stored.

- Size - 20' x 20'
- 400 square feet
- Partial slab foundation
- Building height - 12'-8"
- Ceiling height - 8'
- 6' x 7' sliding side door into storage area
- Material list included

The Oren

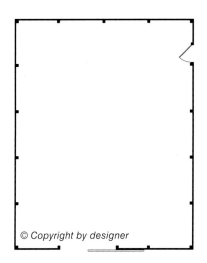

© Copyright by designer

The Oren pole building is a large outbuilding with plenty of space to hold several pieces of farm equipment as well as other items such as vehicles and household items. It features a sliding barn style door on one end and a standard door entry on the opposite corner.

- Size - 32' x 40'
- 1,280 square feet
- Dirt floor foundation
- Building height - 16'
- Ceiling height - 10'
- 10' x 8' sliding door
- Material list included
- Step-by-step instructions

PLAN #F55-133D-7502

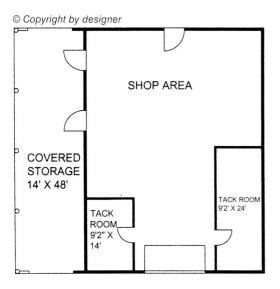

© Copyright by designer

SHOP AREA

COVERED STORAGE 14' X 48'

TACK ROOM 9'2" X 14'

TACK ROOM 9'2' X 24'

- Size - 50' x 48'
- 2,400 square feet
- Slab foundation
- Building height - 20'-2"
- Ceiling heights -
  Tack rooms - 8'
  Shop area - 10'
- 2" x 6" exterior walls

The Heath

The Heath is a roomy workshop with two tack room spaces, a huge shop area plus plenty of outdoor covered storage. It offers plenty of space for the equestrian enthusiast, or for housing other types of farm animals.

PLAN #F55-160D-7501

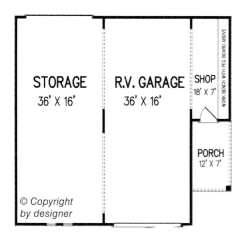

STORAGE 36' X 16'

R.V. GARAGE 36' X 16'

SHOP 18' X 7'

WORK BENCH WITH PEG BOARD ABOVE

PORCH 12' X 7'

© Copyright by designer

- Size - 39' x 36'
- 1,362 total square feet
  Storage - 576
  RV garage - 576
  Shop - 126
  Covered porch - 84
- Slab foundation
- Building height - 25'

The Deltaville

The Deltaville barn offers several great features including an RV garage, a designated shop complete with a work bench with peg board above and a sizable storage area with an easy-access garage door entry. The pleasing covered porch into the shop adds even more curb appeal to this attractive structure.

The Barngat

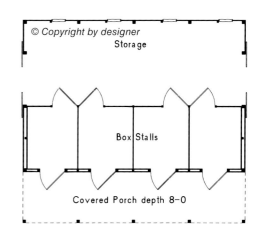

© Copyright by designer
Storage

Box Stalls

Covered Porch depth 8-0

The Barngat horse barn has a large covered porch that connects all four stalls and leads, while there's also a huge storage space for feed, and other supplies. Two 8' x 8' sliding doors and eight 4' x 7' Dutch doors add a variety ways to keep the space well ventilated.

- Size - 36' x 32'.
- 1,152 square feet
- Dirt floor foundation
- Building height - 14'-9"
- Wall height - 9'
- Material list included
- Step-by-step instructions included

The Garfield Farm

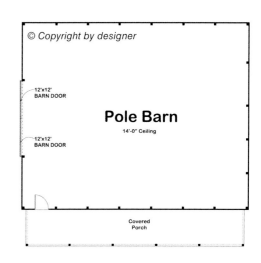

© Copyright by designer

12'x12'
BARN DOOR

Pole Barn
14'-0" Ceiling

12'x12'
BARN DOOR

Covered
Porch

The Garfield Farm pole barn has an expansive covered porch in addition to two 12' x 12' sliding barn doors. With its covered front porch and open interior, it would be the perfect spot for the family handyman to work without any distractions!

- Size - 50' x 30'
- 1,500 square feet
- Slab foundation
- Building height - 20'
- Ceiling height - 14'
- Post frame exterior walls

PLAN #F55-136D-6011

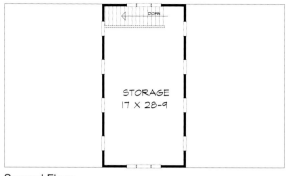

Second Floor
612 sq. ft.

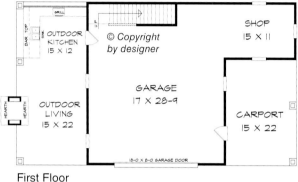

First Floor
1,200 sq. ft.

PLAN #F55-142D-7601

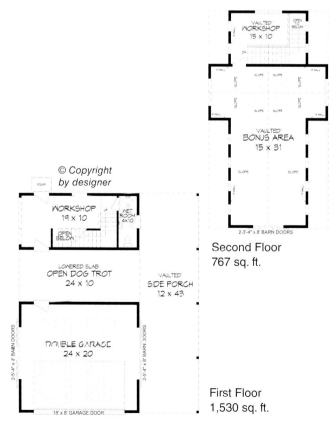

© Copyright
by designer

Second Floor
767 sq. ft.

First Floor
1,530 sq. ft.

The Buckingham Lane

The Buckingham Lane barn has storage, a carport, a 2-car garage with shop, and an outdoor living area with a kitchen and fireplace.

- Size - 61'-10" x 34'
- 2,652 total square feet
  Garage/shop - 1,200
  Storage - 612
  Outdoor liv/kit - 510
  Carport - 330
- Slab foundation
- Building height - 29'
- 2" x 6" exterior walls

The Sonoma Bay

The Sonoma Bay has so much to offer. A dog trot, a vaulted workshop, and a bath are just a few of many highlights.

- Size - 36' x 42'-6"
- 2,297 total square feet
  Workshop - 264
  Garage - 516
  Dog trot - 240
  Side porch - 510
  Bonus area - 767
- Slab foundation
- 1 full bath
- Building height - 30'

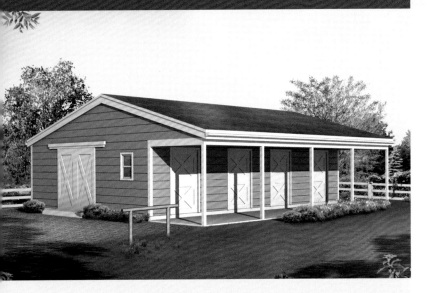

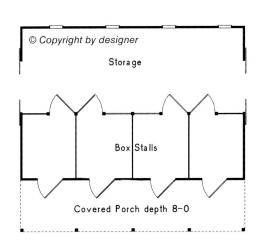

© Copyright by designer

Storage

Box Stalls

Covered Porch depth 8-0

The Barnhart is a four stall horse barn with four doors leading to a covered porch and four doors leading to a storage area. It also has 8' x 7' sliding doors on each end of the building for easy access. Keep your prized equines comfortable and safe in this terrific structure.

- Size - 36' x 24'
- 864 square feet
- Slab foundation
- Building height - 13'-4"
- Ceiling height - 8'
- Material list included

The Pemberville

PLAN #F55-002D-7515

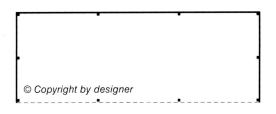

© Copyright by designer

Look no further if you're seeking an open shed pole building! The Pemberville offers great machinery or supply storage that can be lengthened by adding additional 12' bays if needed. Build the perfect sized open air building for your specific needs.

- Size - 36' x 13'
- 468 square feet
- Dirt floor
- 8' or 10' front wall height
- Material list included
- Step-by-step instructions included

PLAN #F55-005D-7500

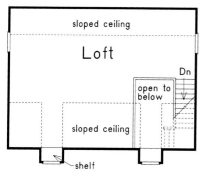

Loft

sloped ceiling

Dn

open to below

sloped ceiling

shelf

Second Floor
525 sq. ft.

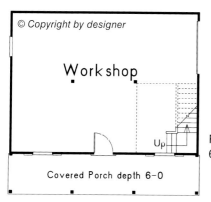

© Copyright by designer

Workshop

Up

First Floor
625 sq. ft.

Covered Porch depth 6-0

PLAN #F55-133D-7512

PULL DOWN STAIRS

ATTIC STORAGE
43' X 15'

Second Floor
704 sq. ft.

EXHAUST FAN

SHOP AREA
© Copyright
by designer

ATTIC TRUSSES ABOVE

FISHING ROOM
12' X 13'

EXHAUST FAN

COVERED PORCH
44' X 6'

First Floor
1,448 sq. ft.

The Tolland Place

The Tolland Place is an open workshop with ample space and a handy loft above. A side garage door makes entry easy.

- Size - 30' x 22'
- 1,150 total square feet -
  First floor - 625
  Second floor - 525
- Slab foundation
- Building height - 20'-6"
- Ceiling heights -
  First floor - 8'
  Second floor - 8'
- Material list included

The Monty

Showcase your favorite hobby in the Monty shed. It has a roomy shop area, a fishing room, a half bath, plus second floor attic storage.

- Size - 44' x 30'
- 2,416 total square feet -
  Shop/fishing room - 1,448
  Covered porch - 264
  Attic storage - 704
- Slab foundation
- 1 half bath
- Building height - 23'-4"
- 2" x 6" exterior walls

The Lang

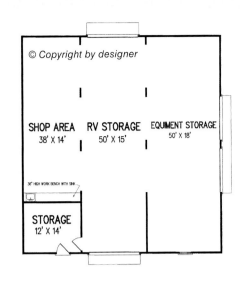

© Copyright by designer

SHOP AREA 38' X 14'

RV STORAGE 50' X 15'

EQUIMENT STORAGE 50' X 18'

36" HIGH WORK BENCH WITH SINK

STORAGE 12' X 14'

The Lang is an attractive barn style structure featuring an RV garage, equipment storage, a shop area with a sink and counter, and a separate storage closet. Perfect for the car enthusiast, or the avid traveler, this barn houses your vehicles safe and sound.

- Size - 48' x 50'
- 2,400 square feet
- Slab foundation
- Building height - 23'

The Chatman

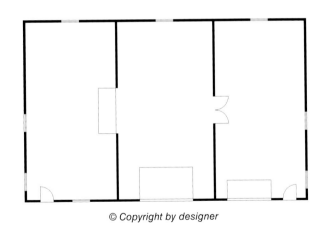

© Copyright by designer

The Chatman barn is designed for easy maintenance and has multiple doors in various sizes for easily storing farm equipment and the other necessities of rural life.

- Size - 64' x 40'
- 2,560 square feet
- Slab foundation
- Building height - 25'-5"
- Ceiling heights -
    Workshop (left) - 10'-7"
    RV garage - 20'-11"
    Garage (right) - 10'-7"
- 2" x 6" exterior walls

PLAN #F55-142D-7606

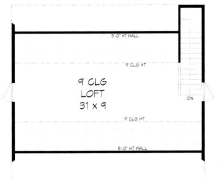

Second Floor
644 sq. ft.

9' CLG
LOFT
31 x 9

5'-0" HT WALL

9' CLG HT

9' CLG HT

5'-0" HT WALL

DN

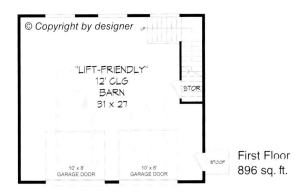

© Copyright by designer

UP

"LIFT-FRIENDLY"
12' CLG
BARN
31 x 27

STOR

10' x 8'
GARAGE DOOR

10' x 8'
GARAGE DOOR

STOOP

First Floor
896 sq. ft.

PLAN #F55-095D-0060

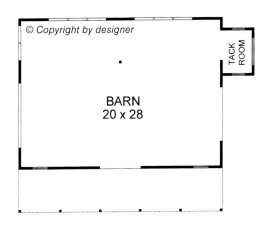

© Copyright by designer

TACK ROOM

BARN
20 x 28

- Size - 27' x 34'
- 918 square feet
- Slab foundation
- Building height - 18'
- Ceiling height - 8'

The Grande Pines

The Grande Pines barn style garage is ideal for holding additional vehicles safely and in today's country style.

- Size - 32' x 28'
- 1,540 total square feet -
  First floor - 896
  Second floor - 644
- Slab foundation
- Building height - 27'-8"
- Ceiling heights -
  First floor - 12'
  Second floor - 9'
- 2" x 6" exterior walls

The Lindy

The Lindy classic homestead style barn is the ideal size to shelter farm animals. Multiple barn style doors provide easy access to and from, and a small tack room keeps all of your equestrian supplies neat and tidy. This would be a great addition to your property!

The Truman Hill

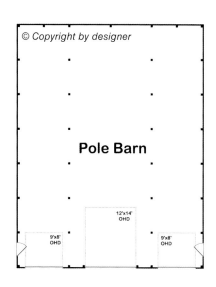

© Copyright by designer

Pole Barn

12'x14'
OHD

9'x8'
OHD

9'x8'
OHD

The Truman Hill is designed for easy maintenance and has multiple doors in various sizes for easily storing farm equipment, an RV, or other vehicles. This classic pole building style would be a great, functional addition to any property or farm.

- Size - 56' x 44'
- 2,464 square feet
- Slab foundation
- Building height - 26'
- Ceiling height - 10'
- Post frame exterior walls

The Nixon Farm

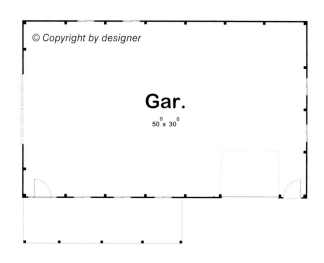

© Copyright by designer

Gar.

50^0 x 30^0

The Nixon Farm barn garage is designed with great Modern Farmhouse style. It is ideal for easy maintenance thanks to its barn style door, perfect for storing large farm equipment or vehicles. An overhead door also helps make storage a breeze, too!

- Size - 50' x 38'
- 1,900 square feet
- Slab foundation
- Building height - 20'
- Ceiling height - 14'
- Post frame exterior walls

Cabana Plans

Plan #F55-126D-1153 on page 110

Cabanas are small structures that often include entertaining space and a bathroom and are usually built with an open side facing a beach or swimming pool. With outdoor living spaces as popular as ever, cabanas can add another element of comfort to your backyard and provide a great sheltered space for entertaining, or just everyday relaxing. These cabana plans come in a variety of styles and sizes perfect pool-side, beach-side, or even in the desert or mountains.

The Cabana Palms Cabana Plan

The Cabana Palms deluxe cabana plan may be small in size, but it's big when it comes to function. Inside, you'll discover a full bath with a roomy walk-in shower topped with a skylight. On the exterior, a covered area has a built-in table for getting out of the sun and cooling off in the shade. There's also a double door storage closet and around the back an alcove for the pool equipment. It's the ideal way to hide unsightly pool equipment while adding function to your swimming pool area.

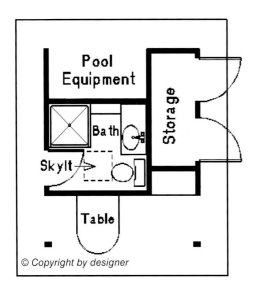

PLAN #F55-002D-4518

- Size - 11' x 13'-6"
- 149 square feet
- Slab foundation
- Building height - 11'-7"
- Ceiling height - 8'
- Material list included
- Step-by-step instructions included

QTY.	SIZE	DESCRIPTION
1 pc.	2x4x12'	Bottom plate (treated)
3 pcs.	2x4x10'	Bottom plate (treated)
2 pcs.	2x4x8'	Bottom plate (treated)
1 pc.	2x4x14'	Top plate
1 pc.	2x4x12'	Top plate, cut
3 pcs.	2x4x10'	Top plate
2 pcs.	2x4x8'	Top plate
2 pcs.	2x4x14'	Tie plate
1 pc.	2x4x12'	Tie plate
3 pcs.	2x4x8'	Tie plate, one cut
4 pcs.*	1x4x12'	Diagonal corner brace
53 pcs.	2x4x8'	Studs
2 pcs.	2x12x8'	Header
3 pcs.	4x4x8'	Posts
4 pcs.	2x4x14'	Trimmer stud, cut
2 pcs.	2x12x12'	Header, cut for 3 pcs.
2 pcs.	4x6x8'	Post
2 pcs.	2x12x12'	Beam
2 pcs.	2x12x8'	Beam, cut for 2 pcs.
11 pcs.	2x6x18'	Rafters, cut for 2 pcs.
2 pcs.	2x8x10'	Hip rafter, cut
8 pcs.	2x6x12'	Jack rafter, header
1 pc.	2x8x12'	Ridge board
10 pcs.	2x6x12'	Ceiling joists
2 pcs.	2x4x12'	Ceiling end blocking
560 sq. ft.	7/16"x8"	Hardboard siding, 6" exposed
2	3'-0"x6'-8"x1 3/4"	Door, solid core
1	2'-6"x6'-8"x1 3/4"	Door, solid core
120 ln. ft.	1x6	Door jamb
120 ln. ft.	1x2	Door trim
1 pc.	1x8x8'	Shelf material, cut
1 set		Shelf standards (metal)
1	36"	Base cabinet with top
11 pcs.	4'x8'x1/2"	Ext. CD 24/0 plywood roof sheathing
90 ln. ft.	1xa8	Fascia and gable fascia
86 ln. ft.	1x4	Frieze/trim at header
7 pcs.	4'x8'x3/8"	Exterior plywood porch ceiling, soffit
100 ln. ft.	1x2	Drip edge, eave and rake
4 sqs.		Roof shingles (self-seal)
1 roll	15#	Roofing felt
320 sq. ft.	1/2"	Drywall (bath walls and ceiling)
3		Key in knob cylinder lock set
6		Door butts hinges with screws
10 lbs.	16d	Common nails, coated, framing
5 lbs.	8d	Common nails, coated, framing, plywood
2 lbs.	8d	Casing nails, coated, trim
5 lbs.	8d	Galvanized siding nails
5 lbs.	1 1/4"	Galvanized roofing nails
1 box	1/2"x12"	Anchor bolts with nuts and washers
210 sq. ft.	6"x6"-2.9x2.9	Wire mesh, slab reinforcing
3 cu. yds.		Ready mix concrete, footing
3 cu. yds.		Ready mix concrete, wall
5 cu. yds.		Ready mix concrete, floor

OPTIONAL MATERIAL

QTY.	SIZE	DESCRIPTION
1 pc.	28"x28"x1/4"	Clear plastic for skylight
1 pc.	1x4x12'	Skylight trim
1 pc.	2x2x12'	Skylight blocking
18		Seismic/hurricane anchor, with nails, bottom plate
18		Seismic/hurricane anchor, with nails, rafters
1 sht.	4'x8'x3/4"	Plywood for table top

*OPTIONAL FOR ALTERNATE CORNER BRACING

QTY.	SIZE	DESCRIPTION
18 shts.	4'x8'x1/2"	Exterior plywood sheathing
5 lbs.	8d	Common nails, coated

The first step in building your cabana is to visit your local building department, present your building plans, and obtain a building permit. A little time spent obtaining the correct information now can save you a lot of grief later.

Plan the placement of the cabana on your lot to conform to local code requirements such as side and rear lot set-backs.

Working with concrete can be tricky for the uninitiated and requires a good deal of assistance. We suggest that you contract this portion of your cabana to a professional.

If concrete is poured by a contractor, omit steps below and start project at wall and roof construction.

Stake out the area as illustrated. Be sure all corners are square. Remember that dimensions on plan are to outside of concrete and to exterior face of stud.

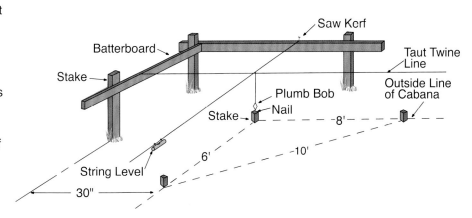

Use details for either NO FROST or FROST CONSTRUCTION depending on your geographical area.

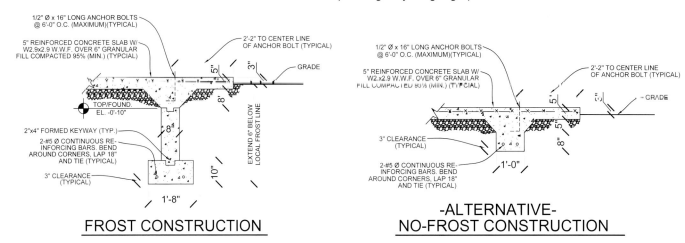

FROST CONSTRUCTION

**-ALTERNATIVE-
NO-FROST CONSTRUCTION**

If building for frost conditions, you must first form the foundation according to the details and layout on the plans. Construct the forms for the concrete using 2" lumber.

NOTE: SETTING AT LEAST TWO 1/2" DIAMETER (OR #4) REINFORCING BARS IN THE THICKENED PORTIONS OF CONCRETE MAKE FOR A MORE SOUND FOUNDATION.

Call building inspector to approve location and formwork prior to pouring concrete.

Once concrete has cured for the foundation you can start the framing for the floor slab. Set the top of 2" form board to desired floor height and level it. Inside face of form boards must line up exactly with "string lines" set at the proper dimensions. Brace securely. This is very important to keep forms from pushing out when concrete is poured.

Use a gravel fill and compact it to within 5" of the top of the form boards.

NOTE PRIOR TO POURING CONCRETE SLAB: Have a local electrical and plumbing contractor install all necessary piping under slab for the electrical and plumbing services.

Use 6"x6"-2.9x2.9 wire mesh in floor slab to minimize cracking.

Call building inspector to check electrical, plumbing and your formwork prior to pouring concrete.

Pour enough ready-mix concrete to completely fill the forms. Surface and level with a long straight board and trowel until smooth.

Set anchor bolts as show on the foundation details above extending at least 2 1/2" above the finished concrete surface.

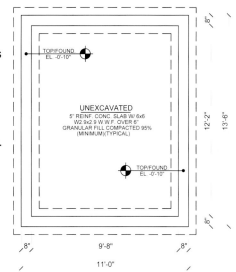

FOUNDATION PLAN

INSTRUCTIONS FOR WALL AND ROOF CONSTRUCTION

After concrete has cured, place 2"x4" bottom plate on top of bolts with edge of 2"x4" 1 3/4" away from the center of the anchor bolts. Tap a hammer over each bolt to locate position of bolt holes. Drill a 3/4" hole at each bolt location in bottom plate. Check for accuracy by placing 2"x4" plate over bolts. Be sure that edge of 2"x4" is flush with the outside face of the wall studs.

Assemble the five exterior wall panels and the top interior wall panels using precut 2"x4" studs 7'-8 5/8" long and 2"x4" top and bottom plates.

The interior wall of the bathroom shower is constructed with 2"x2" studs.

Follow the wall framing elevations. Nail through the top and bottom plate into the 2"x4" stud using two 16 penny nails at the top and at the bottom of each stud. (Note: Do not attach 2"x4" tie plate to top panels yet).

Let-in bracing. Check panels for squareness. Lay the 1"x4" corner brace on panel outer corner at top of panel down to bottom at a 45 degree angle. Mark 1"x4" position on each stud. With your circular power saw cut into studs 3/4" at each mark. Using a chisel and hammer, knock out the pieces of wood leaving a 3/4" recess into which you place the 1"x4" corner brace and nail with two 8 penny nails at each stud and top and bottom plates.

Tilt panel "A" into position. Make sure the all is plumb and square. Secure wall panel to the anchor bolts. (Brace panel as necessary). Follow the same procedure for the remaining wall panels.

Install all headers as shown on the plans. Tie all wall panels together by adding the 2"x4" tie plate to the top of all the wall panels.

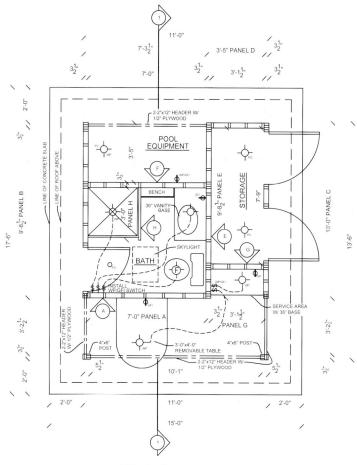

FLOOR PLAN

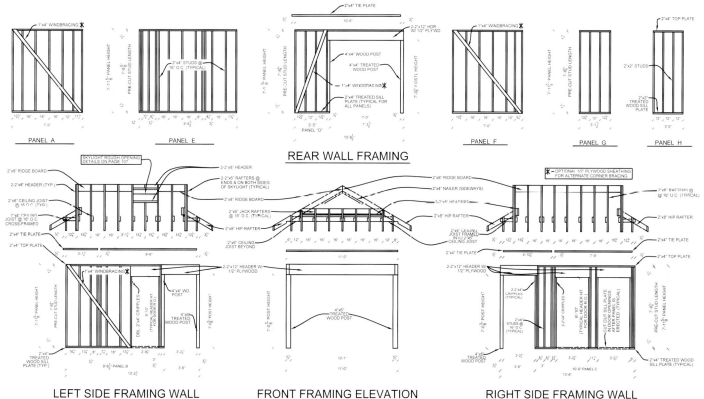

PANEL A   PANEL E   REAR WALL FRAMING   PANEL F   PANEL G   PANEL H

LEFT SIDE FRAMING WALL   FRONT FRAMING ELEVATION   RIGHT SIDE FRAMING WALL

Using the cutting diagram for appropriate roof rafter, cut one of each type and test for fit. Use same rafters to lay out and cut the remaining rafters.

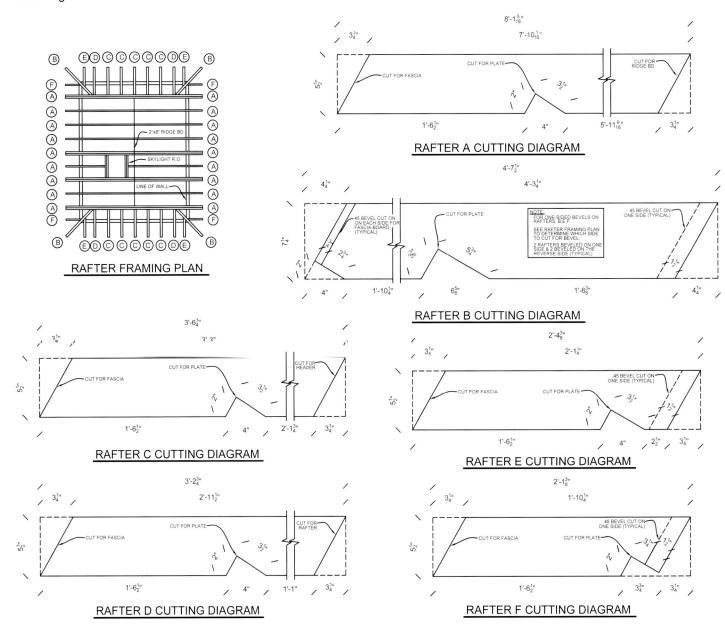

RAFTER FRAMING PLAN

RAFTER A CUTTING DIAGRAM

RAFTER B CUTTING DIAGRAM

RAFTER C CUTTING DIAGRAM

RAFTER E CUTTING DIAGRAM

RAFTER D CUTTING DIAGRAM

RAFTER F CUTTING DIAGRAM

At this time it will be necessary to install 2-2"x8" headers at each end for the hip roof rafters as shown on framing drawings. Nail each rafter in place using 16 penny nails.

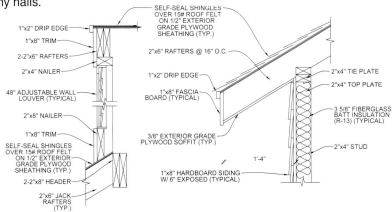

Note: At this time add optional seismic/hurricane anchors per manufacturer's instructions provided with product.

Apply the plywood sheathing to the roof using 6 penny nails spaced 6" o.c.

at the edges and 12" o.c. at the intermediate joists. Cover roof sheathing with 15# roofing felt.

SEISMIC/HURRICANE DETAILS

SKYLIGHT DETAIL

Allowing for 6" exposure, attach 7/16" hardboard siding to exterior walls following the manufacturer's instructions provided with the product.

Install pre-hung doors and optional skylight unit.

Install self-sealing roof shingles following the manufacturer's instructions provided with the product.

Add metal corner moldings to all corners. Install pre-manufactured gable wall louvers. Install all other exterior trim.

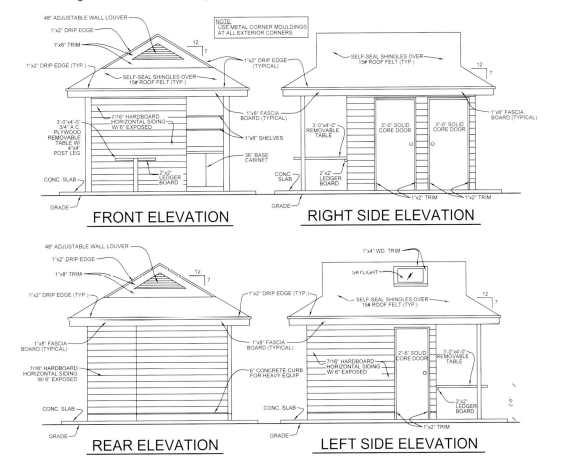

FRONT ELEVATION

RIGHT SIDE ELEVATION

REAR ELEVATION

LEFT SIDE ELEVATION

NOTE: At this time have the plumber and electrician finish all necessary piping and equipment installation prior to the hanging of drywall.

Install 1/2" water resistant drywall to all walls and ceiling in the bathroom.

Tape and sand all seams in dry wall.

Paint all walls and ceiling following instructions provided with product.

Have the plumber and electrician install all fixtures and trim as needed. Note: Bench and vanity base should be made of the same material.

Install service area base cabinet and shelving as desired.

Install removable table. Table top may be either pre-made or constructed using 3/4" AC painted plywood.

Paint or stain siding and trim as desired following manufacturer's instructions provided with the product.

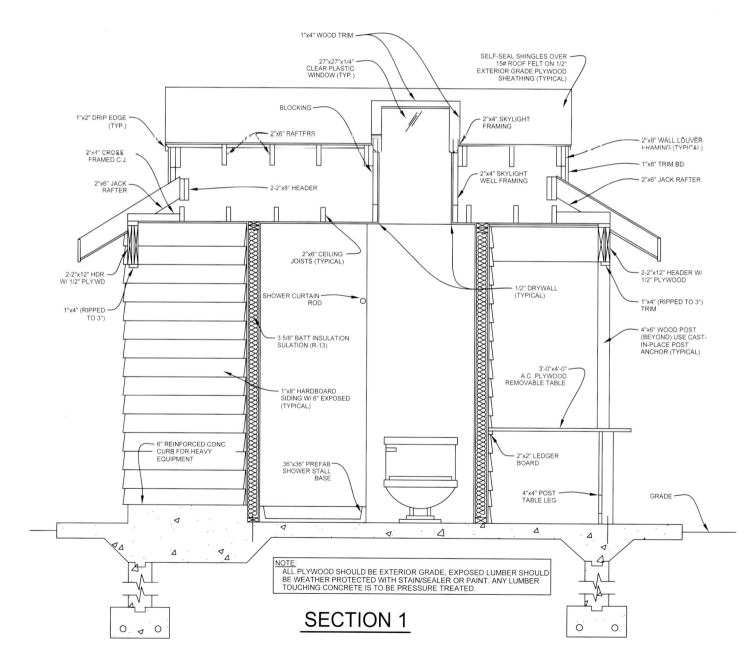

SECTION 1

NOTE:
ALL PLYWOOD SHOULD BE EXTERIOR GRADE, EXPOSED LUMBER SHOULD BE WEATHER PROTECTED WITH STAIN/SEALER OR PAINT. ANY LUMBER TOUCHING CONCRETE IS TO BE PRESSURE TREATED.

PLAN #F55-174D-7501

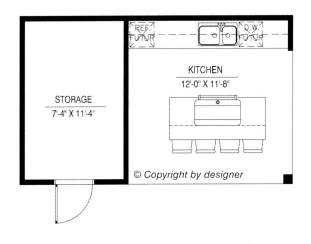

STORAGE
7'-4" X 11'-4"

KITCHEN
12'-0" X 11'-8"

REF. FUTUR

D.W. FUTUR

© Copyright by designer

- Size - 20' x 12'
- 240 square feet
- Slab foundation
- Building height - 12'
- Ceiling height - Sloped ceiling

The Juno

The Juno cabana is the perfect choice for outdoor dining and entertaining since it features an outdoor kitchen with space for a refrigerator, and a large island with a built-in grill. Have fun showing off your cooking skills with a front row seat for family and friends. Extra storage is an added plus, too!

PLAN #F55-142D-7593

© Copyright by designer

STORAGE 5 X 10

WORKSHOP 18 X 14

9 X 7 GARAGE DOOR

PULL-DOWN STAIRS

LIN

SHWR

BATH 6 X 14

STORAGE 17 X 14

9 X 7 GARAGE DOOR

OUTDOOR SHOWER

TV CABINET

SHELVES

VAULTED BAR/ GRILL 11 X 13

VAULTED LANAI 13 X 13

- Size - 24' x 44'-5"
- 1,065 total square feet
  Bar/grill/lanai - 318
  Workshop/storage/bath - 747
- Slab foundation
- 1 full bath
- Building height - 17'-10"
- Ceiling height - 9'

The Carolina Coast

The Carolina Coast cabana has great covered outdoor space perfect for comfortable entertaining, plus tons of indoor storage space. Utilize the workshop for your favorite hobbies, or use the storage and/or workshop space to house extra vehicles.

The Mirage

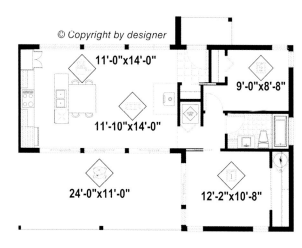

© Copyright by designer

11'-0"x14'-0"

9'-0"x8'-8"

11'-10"x14'-0"

24'-0"x11'-0"

12'-2"x10'-8"

The Mirage cabana cottage has a stylish modern exterior that's hard to ignore. Inside, find a sizable island kitchen with a table extension that seats four, a living area with a wood stove, two bedrooms, and a full bath. Three sets of sliding glass doors across the front give this cabana cottage an open, airy feel.

- Size - 40' x 26'
- 1,040 total square feet
    Cabana - 776
    Covered patio - 264
- Slab foundation
- 2 bedrooms, 1 full bath
- Building height - 21'
- Ceiling height - 9' vaults to 10'
- 2" x 6" exterior walls

The Olsen

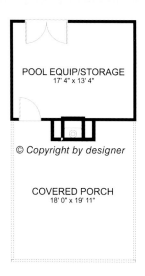

POOL EQUIP/STORAGE
17' 4" x 13' 4"

© Copyright by designer

COVERED PORCH
18' 0" x 19' 11"

The Olsen offers stylish "glamping" in your own backyard and takes shaded outdoor relaxation to a whole new level thanks to its stunning fireplace, chandelier and can lighting. It's the perfect place to unwind in your yard or pool side with grill space, and even a large pool equipment/storage area.

- Size - 18' x 34'
- 612 square feet
- Monolithic slab foundation
- Building height - 16'-9"
- Ceiling height - 10'

PLAN #F55-142D-7595

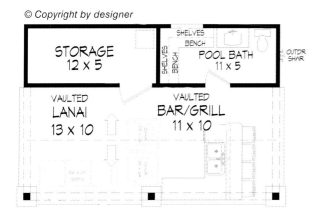

- Size - 24' x 16'
- 384 total square feet
  Lanai/bar/grill - 246
  Bath - 66
  Storage - 72
- Slab foundation
- 1 half bath
- Building height - 17'
- Ceiling height - 10'

The Watershed is the perfect shaded cabana for your pool or yard! There's a roomy half bath with benches for getting ready after a dip in the pool. The vaulted lanai and bar/grill offer plenty of space to party in style. Plus, a sizable storage closet is a welcome extra.

PLAN #F55-125D-7507

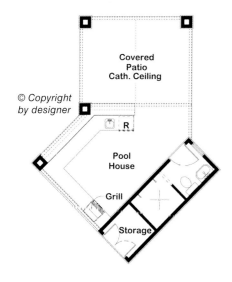

- Size - 25' x 32'
- 475 total square feet
  Pool house/bath/storage - 305
  Covered porch/patio - 170
- Slab foundation
- 1 full bath
- Building height - 17'
- Ceiling height - 9'

The Ivarson pool house has a breezy open-air area with a grill. Nearby is a vaulted covered patio with a cathedral ceiling. There's a full bath for ease when entertaining pool side and changing out of swimming attire. Extra storage can be accessed from the outside for convenience, too.

The Great Cove

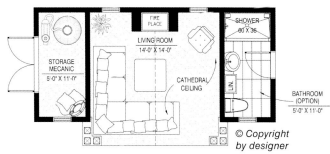

© Copyright by designer

The Great Cove pool-side structure is so fantastic chances are you will enjoy this special escape well into the Fall. The vaulted living room with fireplace is a cozy spot as the cooler months arrive. A full bath and storage are both accessed from the exterior.

- Size - 26' x 12'
- 351 square feet
- Slab foundation
- 1 full bath
- Building height - 18'-6"
- Ceiling height - Cathedral ceiling

The Carefree

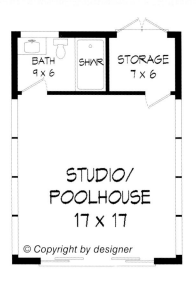

© Copyright by designer

The Carefree cabana studio/pool house is perfect for stepping out of the sun and cooling off. It can also be used as guest, or in-law quarters since it has a full bath and a large storage closet. Transom windows surround the interior ensuring plenty of sunlight inside, while also maintaining privacy.

- Size - 18' x 24'
- 432 total square feet -
    Studio/pool house/bath - 385
    Storage - 47
- Slab foundation
- 1 full bath
- Building height - 14'-6"
- Ceiling height - 10'
- Concrete block exterior walls

PLAN #F55-009D-7527

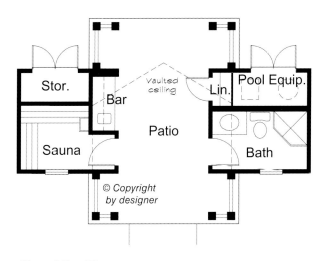

The Summersun

- Size - 26' x 17'
- 442 total square feet
    Bath and sauna - 151
    Patio - 291
- Slab foundation
- 1 full bath
- Building height - 13'
- Ceiling heights -
    Bath and sauna - 8'
    Patio - 10'-8"

The Summersun pool pavilion has a walk-up wet bar, a roomy sauna with a built-in bench, a full bath, and two storage closets to the rear. Create memories all summer long around your pool or patio at this fun vaulted covered patio pavilion!

PLAN #F55-173D-7510

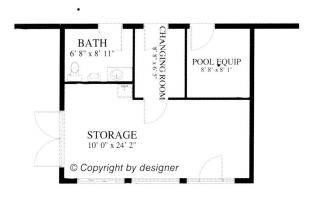

The Allen

- Size - 20'-4" x 25'-4"
- 518 square feet
- Monolithic slab foundation
- 1 half bath
- Building height - 17'-10"
- Ceiling height - 12'
- 2" x 6" exterior walls

The Allen pool-side structure has solid modern style on the outside and comfort and great function on the inside. Step inside from a variety of entries and discover a large storage area, a changing room, a half bath, and a pool equipment closet.

The Harmon Lane

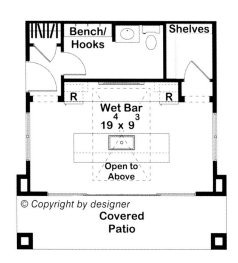

Bench/
Hooks

Shelves

R   R

Wet Bar
19 x 9

Open to
Above

© Copyright by designer

Covered
Patio

The Harmon Lane pool house is great for any pool owner and welcomes all with a large patio door and a covered area that is great for entertaining when the sun reaches its peak. Inside lies a kitchen with a sink and multiple refrigerators to keep your drinks cool. Storage and a half bath offer everything you need!

- Size - 22' x 24'
- 487 total square feet -
     Cabana - 364
     Covered patio - 123
- Slab foundation
- 1 half bath
- Building height - 19'
- Ceiling height - 9'

The Cesar

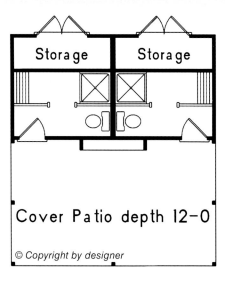

Storage   Storage

Cover Patio depth 12-0

© Copyright by designer

The Cesar pool-side structure has two dressing areas and each have their own bench, shower and toilet. The shady covered patio is ideal for a snack and drink bar. Two storage areas are accessible to the outdoors making them highly convenient for lawn and pool equipment.

- Size - 20' x 22'
- 440 square feet
- Slab foundation
- 2 baths
- Building height - 13'-5"
- Ceiling height - 8'
- Material list included
- Step-by-step instructions included

PLAN #F55-142D-7600

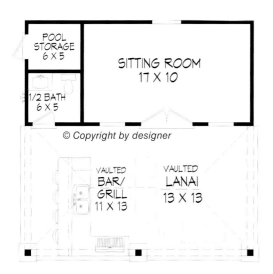

© Copyright by designer

- Size - 24' x 24'
- 576 total square feet
  - Sitting room - 195
  - Half bath - 34
  - Lanai/bar/grill - 318
  - Pool storage - 29
- Slab foundation
- 1 half bath
- Building height - 16'-9"
- Ceiling height - 9'

PLAN #F55-113D-7509

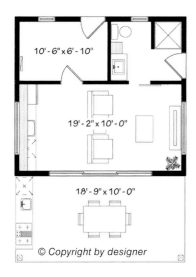

© Copyright by designer

- Size - 28' x 28'
- 784 total square feet
  - Cabana - 360
  - Covered patio - 424
- Monolithic slab foundation standard; floating slab or crawl space foundation available for an additional fee
- 1 bedroom, 1 full bath
- Building height - 16'
- Ceiling height - 8'

The Bahama Breeze

Step out of the blistering sun and cool off in the Bahama Breeze cabana. The open-air vaulted lanai with bar/grill makes any day at the pool a party! The wet bar has a built-in grill with space for four to hangout. Or, seek shelter from the heat in the sitting room. There's even a half bath and storage.

The Rita Beach

The Rita Beach pool cabana is a modern style cabana featuring an outdoor kitchen with plenty of outdoor dining space, a spacious open living area inside, a room perfect as a bedroom, and a full bath. A day at the Rita Beach cabana will be like a mini vacation!

The Sunshine Point

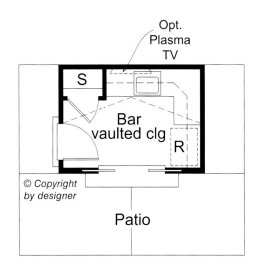

The Sunshine Point cabana is the ideal sheltered bar for a pool deck or hot tub patio offering a counter with storage cabinets, a refrigerator, a designated TV wall, and a storage closet. The serving counter has sliding glass windows and an extended roof overhang for added protection.

- Size - 11' x 8'
- 88 square feet
- Slab foundation
- Building height - 12'
- Ceiling height - 9'-9"

The Summerville

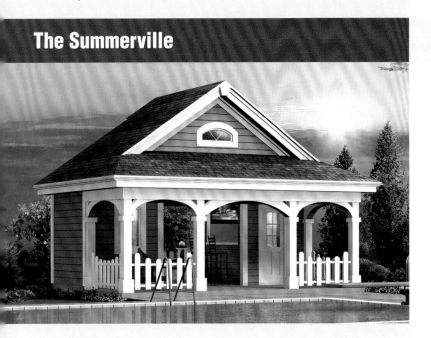

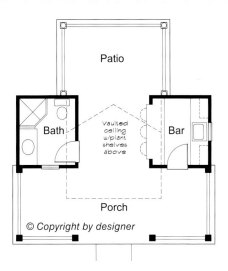

The Summerville pool cabana features a full bath with a walk-in shower, a separate wet bar, and space for three people to hang-out. The vaulted covered porch and a patio complete this adorable pool side cabana. Take a seat, grab a drink, and enjoy life to the fullest!

- Size - 22' x 24'
- 528 total square feet
  Bath and bar - 112
  Patio and porch - 416
- Slab foundation
- 1 full bath
- Building height - 16'-6"
- Ceiling heights -
  Bar and bath - 8'
  Patio - 13'-6"

PLAN #F55-125D-7505

© Copyright by designer

- Size -30' x 24'
- 719 total square feet
  Storage/bath - 182
  Gazebo - 537
- Slab foundation
- 1 half bath
- Building height - 17'
- Ceiling height - 10'

PLAN #F55-009D-7525

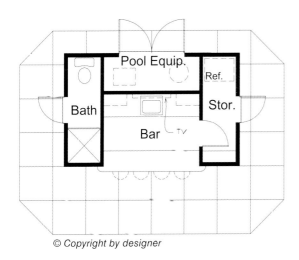

© Copyright by designer

- Size - 16' x 10'
- 160 square feet
- Slab foundation
- 1 full bath
- Building height - 11'
- Ceiling height - 8'

The Marisol Lane

The Marisol Lane welcomes all with large stone columns, a fire pit for cool nights, and even water fountains for that extra designer's touch. The gazebo area is great for entertaining day or night and has a kitchen with a built-in grill, a sink, refrigerator, and buffet area. The niche is great for a TV.

The Coolwater

The Coolwater is the perfect pool companion since it offers a walk-in bar with an open counter, an abundance of cabinets for storage, and a designated wall for a TV. A convenient full bath, a storage room, and rear pool equipment area have also been thoughtfully planned into this design.

The Maxwell Lane

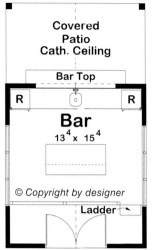

First Floor
224 sq. ft.

Covered Patio
Cath. Ceiling

Bar Top

R | R

Bar
13⁴ x 15⁴

© Copyright by designer

Ladder

Loft
Cath. Ceiling

Optional
Second Floor
224 sq. ft.

The Maxwell Lane plan is a wonderful way to add entertainment value to your home. The covered patio opens up to the bar through a lift-up door. Inside, you'll find a sink, dual refrigerators, a large center island and a stunning loft area.

- Size -14' x 16'
- 224 total square feet
  Bar - 224
  Loft (optional) - 224
- Slab foundation
- Building height - 20'
- Ceiling heights -
  First floor - 8'
  Second floor - 7'

The Shadewell

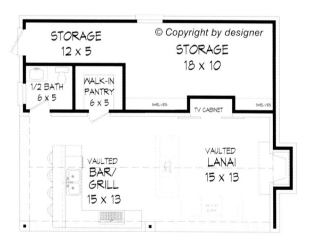

© Copyright by designer

STORAGE
12 x 5

STORAGE
18 x 10

1/2 BATH
6 x 5

WALK-IN PANTRY
6 x 5

SHELVES | TV CABINET | SHELVES

VAULTED
BAR/
GRILL
15 x 13

VAULTED
LANAI
15 x 13

Be comfortable year-round in the Shadewell cabana. With a stone fireplace, this outdoor structure will be comfortable even in the winter. Grab a cold one from the bar/grill and relax in the vaulted lanai with a TV cabinet behind barn-style doors. A half bath, a walk-in pantry, and plenty of storage complete the structure.

- Size - 32' x 24'
- 777 total square feet
  Storage - 256
  Bar/grill/lanai - 444
  Half bath and pantry - 77
- Slab foundation
- 1 half bath
- Building height - 17'-1"
- Ceiling height - 9'

PLAN #F55-125D-7504

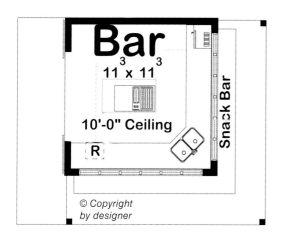

Bar
3 3
11 x 11

10'-0" Ceiling

R

Snack Bar

© Copyright
by designer

- 146 total square feet
- Size - 16' x 16'
- Slab foundation
- Building height - 16'
- Ceiling height - 9'

The Bristol Beach

The Bristol Beach is a stunning backyard structure that will turn your backyard into a tropical paradise with its large outdoor snack bar. The Bristol Beach includes an indoor cook top, a refrigerator, and a double basin sink so party time is anytime!

PLAN #F55-125D-7512

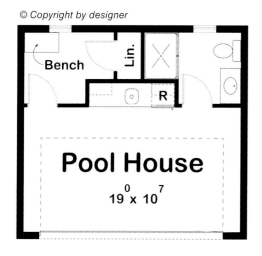

© Copyright by designer

Bench

Lin.

X

R

Pool House
0 7
19 x 10

- Size - 20' x 18'
- 360 square feet
- Slab foundation
- 1 full bath
- Building height - 13'
- Ceiling height - 9'

The Alvarado Vista

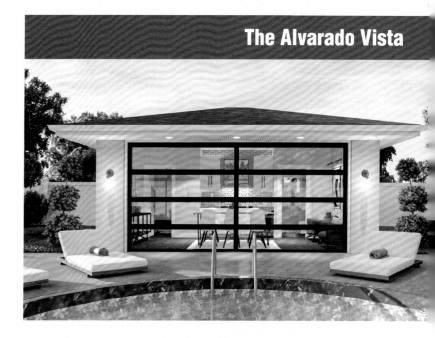

The Alvarado Vista invites all guests through a large front facing garage door. Centered in the middle of the pool house is a bar equipped with a sink and refrigerator space. This unique design gives owners a storage place for towels and other belongings in the "locker room" area as well as a full bath close by.

KITCHENETTE
14 X 10

STORAGE
9 X 9

© Copyright
by designer

PORCH
14 X 6

BATH
9 X 6

SHWR
39x39

Little but mighty, the Duck Island cabana has the essentials for relaxation and fun. The open-air wrap-around porch has a kitchenette ready to whip up a batch of daiquiris at a moment's notice. There's a full bath for added convenience when swimming or partying. Plus, the extra storage is always helpful.

- Size - 24' x 16'
- 384 total square feet
  Kitchenette/porch - 234
  Bath - 65
  Storage - 85
- Slab foundation
- 1 full bath
- Building height - 15'-9"
- Ceiling height - 10'

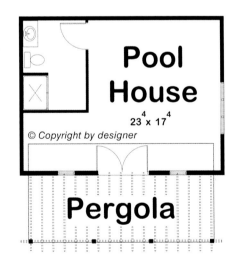

Pool House
23⁴ x 17⁴

© Copyright by designer

Pergola

The Tranquility Lane is everything its name has to offer. Greet guests under the unique pergola design, and it will be obvious this pool house is more than just a storage space. The patio is great for entertaining and sun bathing, but step inside the French doors and find a space where the possibilities are endless.

- Size - 24' x 26'
- 432 square feet
- Slab foundation
- 1 full bath
- Building height - 18'
- Ceiling height - 9'

PLAN #F55-125D-7502

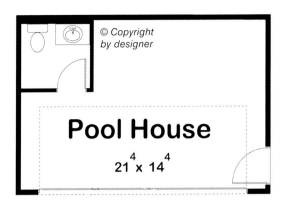

© Copyright by designer

Pool House
21⁴ x 14⁴

- Size - 22' x 15'
- 330 total square feet
- Slab foundation
- 1 half bath
- Building height - 12'
- Ceiling height - 9' sloped

The Raburn Contemporary pool house design is great for all outdoor seekers with its low pitched roof that still provides many opportunities for natural sunlight. The large garage door brings the outdoors inside while escaping the sun on a hot summer day. A half bath is conveniently located in the rear corner.

PLAN #F55-142D-7612

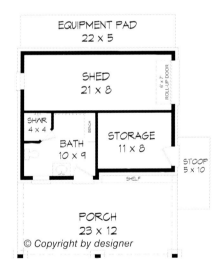

EQUIPMENT PAD
22 x 5

SHED
21 x 8

6' x 7' ROLL-UP DOOR

SHWR
4 x 4

BATH
10 x 9

STORAGE
11 x 8

STOOP
5 x 10

SHELF

PORCH
23 x 12

© Copyright by designer

- Size - 22' x 29'
- 636 total square feet
    - Bath - 101
    - Covered porch - 256
    - Storage and shed - 279
- Slab foundation
- 1 full bath
- Building height - 19'
- Ceiling height - 9'
- 2" x 6" exterior walls

The Rollingwood is comprised of several spaces including a large garage shed space with a roll-up door, a separate storage area with its own stoop, an oversized full bath with a built-in bench, and a large covered porch area perfect for a breezy outdoor living area with a TV shelf.

The Welsh

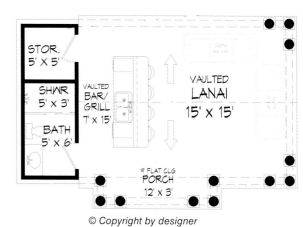

© Copyright by designer

The Welsh is the perfect sized cabana if you want some space for relaxing in the shade, but don't want a large structure. The vaulted lanai has a centered island bar/grill area. Plus, there's a storage closet as well as a full bath with a large walk in shower.

- Size - 28' x 18'-10"
- 492 square feet
- Slab foundation
- 1 full bath
- Building height - 14'
- Ceiling height - 9'

The Miles Beach

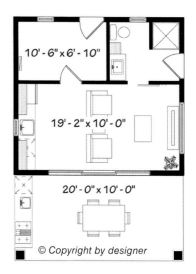

© Copyright by designer

The stylish Miles Beach cabana has an outdoor kitchen with a grill, range, refrigerator, and sink for easy entertaining. Inside, find a kitchenette, full bath, and a bedroom. Whether utilized pool side as a cabana or as guest quarters, the Miles Beach is the perfect departure from the ordinary.

- Size - 28' x 20'
- 560 total square feet
  Cabana - 360
  Covered porch - 200
- Monolithic slab foundation standard; floating slab or crawl space available for an additional fee
- 1 bedroom, 1 full bath
- Building height - 14'-4"
- Ceiling height - 8'

Playhouse Plans

Plan #F55-002D-4514 on page 132

There's nothing quite like the outdoor adventures that are created by children all throughout the summer. Building a children's playhouse will provide just the backdrop for many fun and imaginative days in the great outdoors. Choose from several different children's playhouse plans and soon your kids will be creating an outdoor world of their own designed especially for them.

The Merrill Playhouse Plan

Attractive window boxes on each side window, three operable windows, and a 2' deep covered front porch make this shed playhouse so life-like and charming! With a ceiling height of 6'-1", the kids will love it in the warmer months when they're playing house with their neighborhood friends.

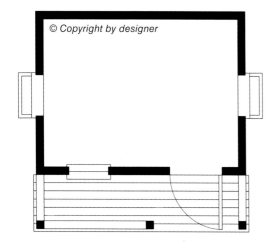

© Copyright by designer

PLAN #F55-002D-4505

- Size - 8' x 8'
- 64 total square feet
- Wood floor on 4x4 runners foundation
- Building height - 9'-2"
- Ceiling height - 6'-1"
- 2' deep covered porch
- Material list included
- Step-by-step instructions included

QTY.	SIZE	DESCRIPTION
FLOOR FRAMING		
1/4 cu. yd.		Gravel
3 pcs.	4x4x8' treated	Floor runners
2 pcs.	2x4x8' treated	Band boards
9 pcs.	2x4x8' treated	Floor joists
1 pc.	2x4x8' treated	Floor blocking
2 shts.	4x8x3/4" ext. plywood	Floor decking
7 pcs.	1x4x10' treated	Floor decking
WALL FRAMING		
3 pcs.	4x4x8'	Posts
15 pcs.	2x4x12'	Wall studs
2 pcs.	2x4x12'	Wall plates
2 pcs.	2x4x10'	Wall headers
8 pcs.	2x4x8'	Wall plates
3 pcs.	2x4x8'	Post plates
ROOF FRAMING		
7 pcs.	2x4x12'	Truss top chords
7 pcs.	2x4x8'	Truss bottom chords
2 pcs.	2x4x12'	Truss king posts & siding nailers
3 pcs.	2x4x12'	Box rakes
1 pc.	2x4x12'	Front gable end
5 shts.	4x8x1/2" ext. plywood	Roof sheathing
1 sht.	4x8x1/2" ext. plywood	Front gable sheathing
DOORS, WINDOWS, SHUTTERS,		
PLANTER BOXES & WOOD VENTS		
2 pcs.	1x6x8'	Door jamb (ripped)
2 pcs.	1x2x8'	Door stop
1 pc.	1x8x8'	Door trim
2 pcs.	1x4x10'	Door trim
3 pcs.	2x2x8'	Window frame
4 pcs.	1/2"x1/2"x12'	Plexiglass stop
3 pcs.	1'-3"x1'-7"x3/16"	Plexiglass
3 pcs.	1x8x0'	Window jamb (ripped)
3 pcs.	3/4"x3/4"x1/2" ext. plywood	Window stop
1 sht.	4x8x1/2" ext. plywood	Shutters
5 pcs.	1x2x8'	Shutters
1 pc.	1x2x8'	Planter boxes
1 pc.	1x8x8'	Planter boxes
1 pc.	1x4x8'	Planter boxes
1 pc.	6"x3' aluminum screen	Planter boxes
2 pcs.	1x2x8'	Wood vents
2 pcs.	1/2"x1/2"x8'	Wood vents
1 sht.	4x8x1/2" ext. plywood	Wood vents
2 pcs.	2'x5' aluminum screen	Wood vents

QTY.	SIZE	DESCRIPTION
FINISH AND TRIM		
4 bundles	-	Asphalt shingles
1 roll	-	15# roofing felt
1 pc.	10"x10'	Metal flashing
5 pcs.	4 1/2"x10'	Metal drip edge
180 l.f.	12"	Tri-lap hardboard siding
1 sht.	4x8x1/2" ext. plywood	Porch ceiling
1 pc.	1x4x8'	Window trim
3 pcs.	1x2x8'	Window trim
2 pcs.	1x4x8'	Door trim
4 pcs.	1x4x12'	Corner boards
4 pcs.	1x6x12'	Fascia boards
4 pcs.	1x2x12'	Trim boards
1 pc.	1x6x14'	Skirt board
1 pc.	1x8x8'	Post wrap
1 pc.	5/4x6x14'	Post wrap
5 pcs.	2x2x8'	Balusters & railing
2 pcs.	1x4x8'	Top railings
2 gal.	-	Paint or stain
2 tubes	-	Caulk
KANT-SAG HARDWARE		
80 ea.	5x3 1/8	S201 Nail-on plates
3 ea.	-	DB44 Post anchors
14 ea.	-	RT7 Truss ties
12 ea.	-	JA1 Railing angles
MISCELLANEOUS HARDWARE		
8 lbs.	16d	Cement coated nails
1 lb.	8d	Cement coated nails
4 lbs.	8d	Galvanized nails
1 lb.	6d	Galvanized nails
6 lbs.	7/8"	Roofing nails
1 lb.	1/4"	Finishing nails
1 lb.	2 1/2"	Galvanized screws
2 lbs.	2"	Galvanized screws
1 lb.	1 1/2"	Galvanized screws
2 tubes	-	Carpenter's glue
6 ea.	3"	Hinges with screws
2 ea.	4"	Hinges with screws
1 ea.	4"	Door pull

1. Study the plan thoroughly and read all the instructions before starting the construction of the playhouse. Be sure to check your local code requirements and obtain a building permit if necessary.

SITE PREPARATION AND RUNNER PLACEMENT

2. Select a location that is level and slightly larger than the playhouse.

3. Dig (3) trenches approximately 8' wide, 9'-0" long, and 2" deep as shown in details A2 and B2. Fill each trench with gravel to the top of the grade. Packing or rolling the gravel will result in a more level base.

4. Cut (3) treated 4x4 runners 8'-0" long. Miter both ends of the 4x4's as shown in detail C2. Position the runners on the gravel trenches and ensure that they are square by measuring the corners. Diagonal dimensions should equal 11'-3 3/4". See detail A2.

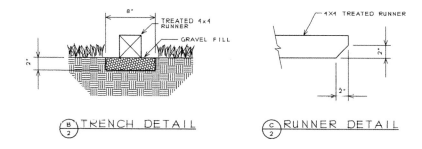

A1 TRENCH AND RUNNER LAYOUT   B2 TRENCH DETAIL   C2 RUNNER DETAIL

FLOOR FRAMING

5. Select (2) treated 2x4's 8'-0" long to use as band boards. Cut (9) 2x4 treated floor joists 7'-9" long. Nail the band boards to the joists using (2) 16d cc (16 penny cement coated) nails per joist at each end as shown in detail D2.

6. Position the 2x4 floor framing on the 4x4 runners. Toenail 16d cc nails through each side of the 2x4 joists into the 4x4's.

7. Once the floor system is attached, nail (3) 2x4 blocks as shown in detail D2. This is needed for support under each porch post.

8. Check to ensure floor system is level and square.

9. Cut (1) 2'-0" x 8'-0" sheet of 3/4"plywood. Fasten the plywood to the 2x4 floor using 8d cc nails spaced 6" apart as shown in detail E2.

10. Cut (7) treated 1x4 boards 8'-2 1/2" long for the porch decking. Attach the boards to each 2x4 joist with (2) 2" galvanized screws allowing a 1 1/4" overhang at the end of each board as shown in detail E2 and F2.

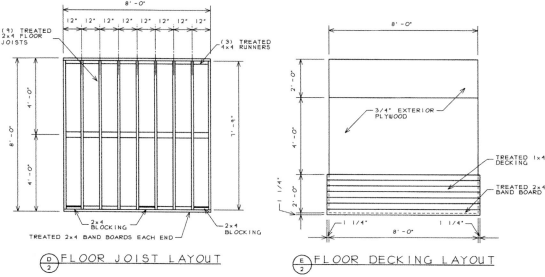

D2 FLOOR JOIST LAYOUT   E2 FLOOR DECKING LAYOUT

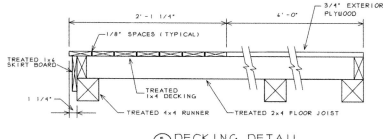

F2 DECKING DETAIL

WALL FRAMING

11. Use the playhouse floor as a work surface to construct the walls and trusses.

12. Cut studs, plates, and headers for the (4) wall panels as follows:

STUDS		PLATES		HEADER	
Qty.	Length	Qty.	Length	Qty.	Length
(26)	5'-9"	(1)	8'-0"	(2)	2'-5"
(2)	4'-11 1/2"	(2)	7'-8 1/2"	(9)	1'-8"
(3)	2'-3 1/2"	(5)	7'-5"		
(3)	1'-1"	(4)	6'-0"		
(1)	6 1/2"				

13. Assemble the (4) wall panels as shown below. Nail the 2x4 top and bottom plates to the studs using (2) 16d cc nails per stud at each end. Attach the headers in the same manner. Lay the panels aside.

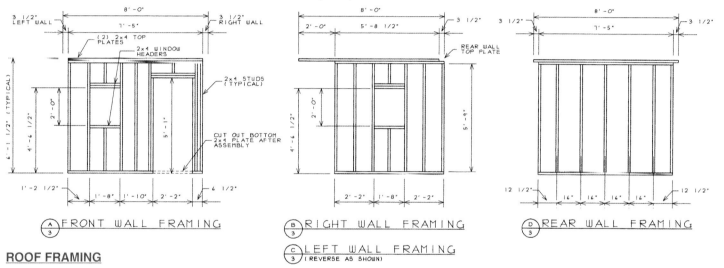

ROOF FRAMING

14. Cut 2x4 chords and webs as shown in detail E3. Build (7) trusses using "S201" nail on plates with a minimum of (3) 7/8" roofing nails per board. Four plates should be used on each side of the truss. The (2) gable end trusses will need (8) additional plates each.

BOX RAKES

15. After assembling the trusses, (4) top chords should be left for the construction of the box rakes.

16. Cut (20) 2x4 blocks 6 1/2" long, (2) 2x4 spacers 11" long, and (2) triangular pieces of screen 4'-6" long and 1'-6" high.

17. Nail the screen to the top chords of the gable ends using 7/8" roofing nails as shown in detail H3.

18. Nail the 2x4 blocks to the top chords using 16d cc nails. Nail the remaining (4) top chords to the 2x4 blocks. Cut and fasten 1/2" plywood to the underside of the box rakes using 6d galvanized nails spaced 6" apart.

WOOD VENTS

19. Nail a 2x4 spacer to the 2x4 king post using 8d nails as shown in detail H3.

20. Cut 1/2" plywood, 1/2" stop, and 1x2 trim for the (2) wood vents as indicated in detail F3. Use carpenter's glue and 1 1/4" finishing nails to assemble the vents. Screw the wood vent to the 2x4 spacer with 2 1/2" galvanized screws.

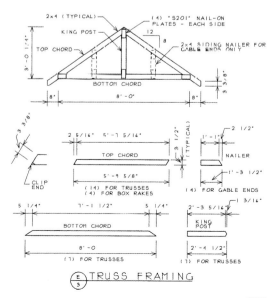

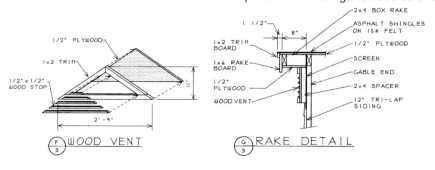

ERECTING THE WALLS

19. Nail a 2x4 spacer to the 2x4 king post using 8d nails as shown in detail H3.

20. Cut 1/2" plywood, 1/2" stop, and 1x2 trim for the (2) wood vents as indicated in detail F3. Use carpenter's glue and 1 1/4" finishing nails to assemble the vents. Screw the wood vent to the 2x4 spacer with 2 1/2" galvanized screws.

ERECTING THE WALLS

21. Position the wall panels in place on the wood floor as shown in detail A4. Temporary bracing may be necessary. Make sure the walls are plumb and square. Secure the wall panels to the floor using 16d cc nails. Nail the panels together at the corners.

4x4 PORCH POSTS

22. Screw (3) DB44 anchors to the 1x4 decking with 2" galvanized screws as shown in detail B4. Cut (3) 4x4 posts 5'-9" long, (2) 2x4 top plates 8'-0" long, and (1) 2x4 top plate 7'-5" long. Nail the (3) 2x4 top plates to the 4x4 posts with 16d cc nails as shown in detail A4. Fasten the 4x4's in the post anchors. Make sure the posts are plumb and square. Nail the right and left wall top plate to the post plates.

ERECTING THE TRUSSES

23. Mark the top plates on the front and rear walls for the location of the trusses indicated in detail C4. Fasten the "RT7" truss ties with 8d cc nails to the top plates as shown in detail D4. Set the trusses one at a time on the top of the wall, fastening the trusses to the ties.

ROOF PLYWOOD

24. Nail a 2x4 block 14 1/2" long between the top chord trusses as shown in detail A4.

25. Measure and cut 1/2" plywood so the joints stagger on the roof. Allow a 3/4" overhang at the edge of the top chords to cover the 1x6 fascia as shown in detail G5. Fasten the plywood to the trusses with 8d cc nails spaced 6" apart.

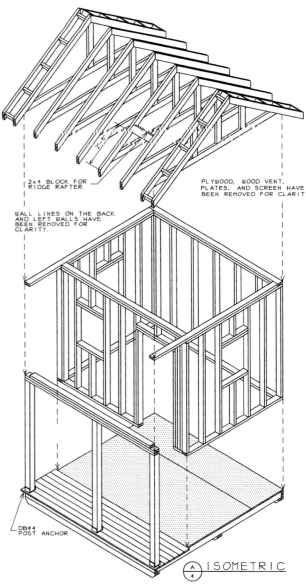

GABLE END DETAIL

ISOMETRIC

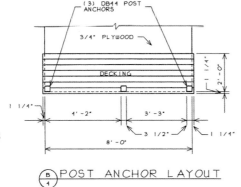

POST ANCHOR LAYOUT

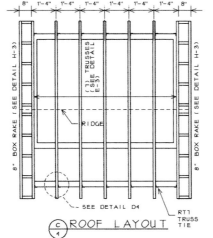

ROOF LAYOUT

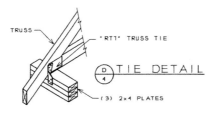

TIE DETAIL

FRONT GABLE FRAMING

26. Cut the 2x4 chords and ridge board as indicated in detail E4. Build (1) front gable truss using "S201" nail-on plates with a minimum of (2) 7/8" roofing nails per board. Three plates should be used on each side of the truss. Fasten 1/2" plywood and plywood applique to the face of the front gable with 8d galvanized nails as shown in detail E4.

27. Position the front gable truss on top of the plywood roof as shown in detail E5. Nail the 2x4 ridge board to the back of the front gable truss and to the 2x4 block. Add 1/2" plywood to the top of the front gable allowing the plywood to hang over the truss 3/4" to cover the 1x6 fascia board.

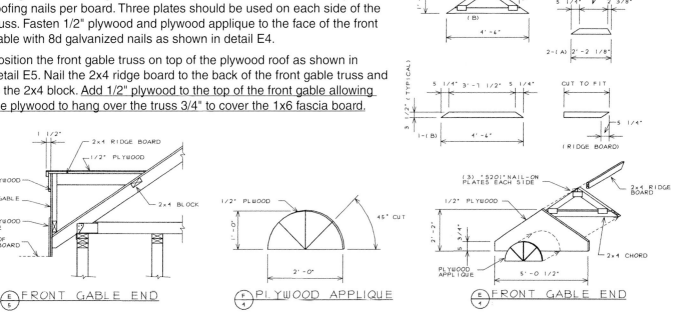

FINISHED ROOFING

28. Apply the 15# roofing felt with 7/8" roofing nails. Start at the bottom of the roof and overlap the felt 4".

29. Apply the flashing on both sides of the front gable as shown in detail A5 and B5. Measure, cut, and attach 1x6 fascia boards, 1x2 trim, and metal drip edge as shown above.

30. Apply the roof shingles per manufacturer's instructions.

SIDING

31. Cut 12" hardboard siding to size for each wall as indicated in the wall elevations below. Start the first row 1 1/2" up from the bottom of the 4x4 runners, making sure the siding is level. Fasten the siding with (2) 8d galvanized nails at every stud.

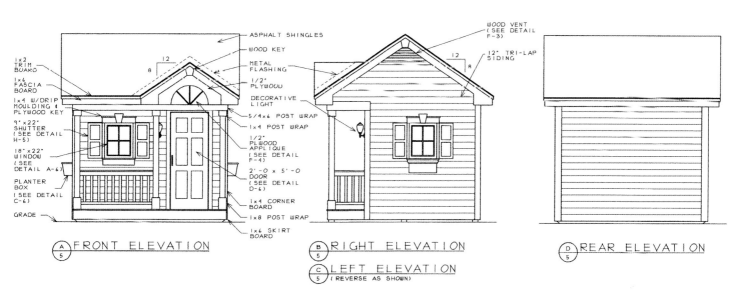

DOOR

32. Check actual door opening with the dimensions in detail D6. Minor adjustments may have to be made to the door dimensions. Measure and cut 1x6 door jamb as shown in detail D6.

33. Measure and cut the 1x4, 1x8, and 3/4" plywood for the door. Glue and screw boards to the backside of the 3/4" plywood using 1 1/2" screws. Attach the hinges and hang the door. Nail the 1x4 door trim in place.

WINDOWS, SHUTTERS AND PLANTER BOXES

34. All (3) windows are constructed in the same manner. Check actual window openings with the dimensions in detail B6, making sure the windows will fit properly.

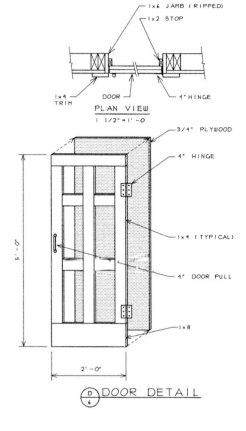

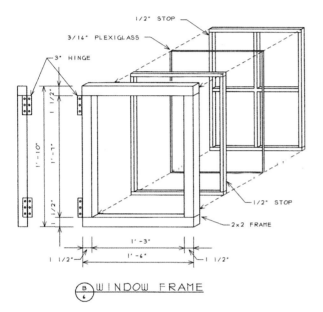

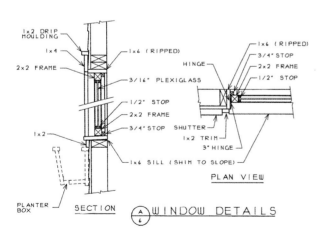

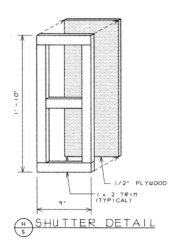

35. Frame out the sides and top of the window openings with ripped 1x6 boards as shown in detail A6. The 1x6 sill should slope slightly.

36. Cut the 2x2 window frame and screw together at the top and bottom with 2 1/2" screws. Tack 1/2" stop to the 2x2's with 1 1/4" finishing nails. Measure and cut the 3/4" window stop, and attach with 6d galvanized nails.

37. Measure and cut 1x2 and 1x4 window trim, 1x2 drip moulding, and plywood keys as shown in detail A6 and E6. Fasten the materials to the siding with 8d galvanized nails.

38. Construct the (6) shutters with carpenter's glue and 1 1/4" finishing nails as shown in detail H5. Screw in place on each side of the windows with 2 1/2" galvanized screws.

39. Construct the (3) planter boxes with carpenter's glue and 1 1/4" finishing nails as shown in detail C6. Screw in place below the windows with 2 1/2" galvanized screws.

FINISH AND TRIM

40. Measure and cut 1x4 comer boards and 1x6 skirt board as shown on elevation A5. Cut gable end keys as shown in detail E6. Fasten in place with 8d galvanized nails.

41. Wrap posts with 1x8 boards as shown in detail A5.

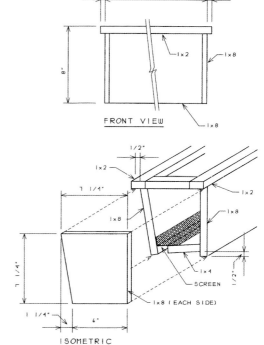

FRONT VIEW

ISOMETRIC

PLANTER DETAIL

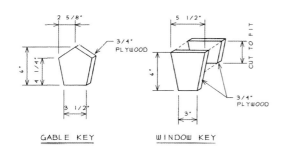

GABLE KEY   WINDOW KEY

PLYWOOD KEYS

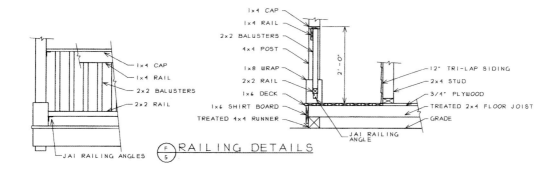

RAILING DETAILS

42. Construct railing as shown in detail F5, spacing balusters a maximum of 4" apart. Fasten the top rails to the balusters with 6d galvanized nails and the bottom rails to the balusters with 2 1/2" galvanized screws. Apply the "JA1" angles to the bottom side of each rail, and attach to the 4x4 posts.

43. Measure and cut plywood soffit above deck as shown in detail G5. Fasten the plywood with 6d galvanized nails. Apply post wrap with 8d galvanized nails.

44. Paint and/or stain as desired per manufacturer's instructions.

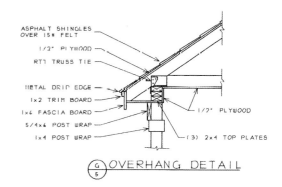

OVERHANG DETAIL

The Sellersville

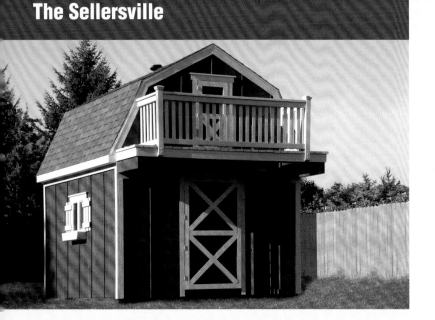

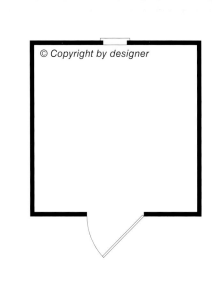

© Copyright by designer

The Sellersville playhouse partners with adolescent fun-time by offering a storage solution that can also be used as a children's playhouse featuring a cute outdoor balcony and a ladder to the loft above. This shed playhouse puts the fun in "fun"ction!

- Size - 12' x 12' with 2'-8" deep balcony
- 144 square feet
- Concrete slab or wood deck on gravel foundation
- Building height - 14'-1"
- Ceiling height - 7'-4"
- 4' x 6'-10" door
- Material list included
- Step-by-step instructions included

The Petunia Lane

PLAN #F55-125D-4514

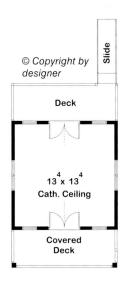

© Copyright by designer

Slide

Deck

13⁴ x 13⁴
Cath. Ceiling

Covered Deck

The Petunia Lane is a fun place that includes space underneath for a porch swing, or even a sandbox. The space itself has a cathedral ceiling, but could be the coolest backyard playhouse ever. A deck off the back includes a fun slide.

- Size - 14' x 24'
- 178 square feet
- Post and pier foundation
- Building height - 22'
- Ceiling height - 8'

PLAN #F55-066D-3000

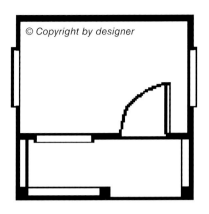

© Copyright by designer

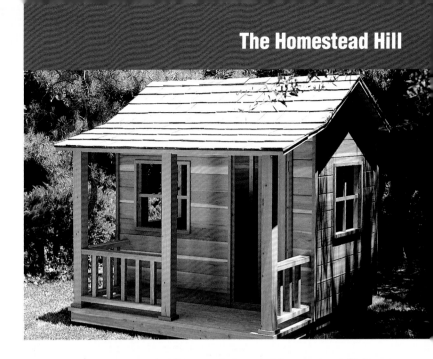

- Size - 6' x 6'
- 36 square feet
- Wood deck on gravel foundation
- Building height - 6'
- Ceiling height - 4'-6"
- Material list included
- Step-by-step instructions included

The Homestead Hill rustic log cabin style children's playhouse is a great carpentry project that is easy-to-follow. Your children and your yard will be a favorite of the neighborhood when the kids can play in their very own child-sized log cabin and pretend like it's the olden days.

PLAN #F55-142D-4500

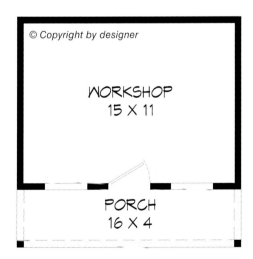

© Copyright by designer

WORKSHOP
15 X 11

PORCH
16 X 4

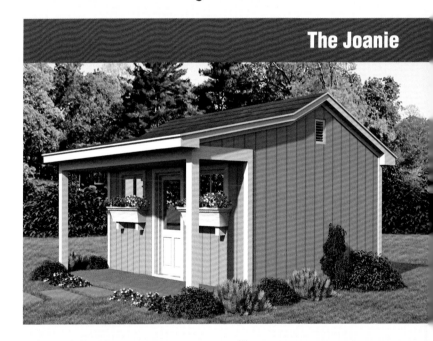

- Size - 16' x 16'
- 256 total square feet
    - Workshop - 192
    - Covered porch - 64
- Slab foundation
- Building height - 11'-4"
- Ceiling height - 8'

The Joanie shed/playhouse is the perfect option for a garden workshop or "she" shed if the kids don't want to make it into their own adorable playhouse! A covered front porch and double window boxes take its charm quotient to a whole new level.

The Daisy Hill

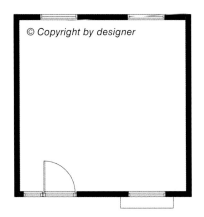

© Copyright by designer

The Daisy Hill is a stunning Modern Farmhouse style structure. The exterior features contrasting white siding with black soffit and fascia. The interior could be a comfortable way to work remotely from home while keeping your home life separate, or build it and create an adorable playhouse for the kids.

- Size - 14' x 14'
- 196 square feet
- Slab foundation
- Building height - 15'
- Ceiling height - 9'

The Shay

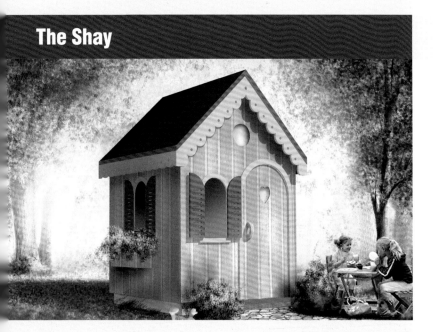

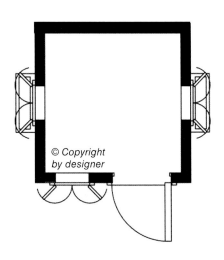

© Copyright by designer

Build the Shay gingerbread style Fairy-tale playhouse and bring back memories of all of those classic and timeless stories you remember as a child. Or, create a fun wonderland for your kids or grandkids where they can truly create lasting memories of fun sunny days.

- Size - 4' x 4'
- 16 square feet
- Wood floor on concrete blocks foundation
- Building height - 12'-6"
- Ceiling height - 8'
- Construction prints are 8 1/2" x 11" in size

Outdoor Project Plans

Plan #F55-066D-0023 on page 143

If you're looking to build a bench for your children that can be passed down for generations, or you want to make your outdoor space beautiful, comfortable and custom, these do-it-yourself outdoor projects include many great functional options that the whole family can help build. Teach everyone something hands-on that they can build and be proud of season after season.

The Willow Breeze
Garden Swing with Canopy Plan

The attractive Willow Breeze wooden garden swing with canopy is sure to be a favorite backyard spot where everyone will want to gather and swing away when the summertime air is humid. Partially shaded from the sun with the pergola style canopy above, this swing will offer a breezy spot in the backyard to relax any time day or night. You can easily build this swing with the step-by-step instructions included.

PLAN #F55-002D-0012

- Sizes -
  Canopy - 12' x 5' x 7'-6" high
  Bench - 6' wide
- This attractive design features a sun-screen canopy styled like a pergola made of sturdy wood
- This is the perfect way to enjoy the outdoors in style and comfort near a patio, or build near a grove of trees for a beautiful backdrop and even more extra shade
- Material list included
- Step-by-step instructions included

NOTE: All lumber to be pressure treated. All metal fasteners are to be galvanized.

QTY.	SIZE	DESCRIPTION
2 ea.		Solid concrete brick
5 bags	90#	Ready mix concrete
2 bags		Gravel fill
2 pcs.	4x4x10'	Posts
1 pc.	4x4x12'	Beam
2 pcs.	2x6x8'	Roof supports, cut
2 pcs.	2x4x12'	Roof supports
2 pcs.	2x6x12'	Roof supports
1 pc.	1x8x8'	End cap, cut
25 pcs.	2x2x8'	Roof slats
35 l.f.	5/8"	Rope
1 tube		Wood glue
1 gal.		Ext. paint or stain/sealer

MISCELLANEOUS HARDWARE

QTY.	SIZE	DESCRIPTION
2 ea.		Metal post and beam cap
2 ea.	3/4"	Drop forge steel/nylon bushing
		Swing hanger (pre-manufactured)
4 ea.	1/2" dia.x4"	Galvanized carriage bolts
2 ea.	1/2" dia.x8"	Galvanized carriage bolts
2 lbs.	#6x2 1/2"	Galvanized wood screws, roof slats
2 lbs.	#8x2 1/2"	Galvanized wood screws, frame

BENCH SWING

QTY.	SIZE	DESCRIPTION
1 pc.	2x6x12'	Bench frame
1 pc.	2x4x8'	Bench arm rest
1 pc.	1x6x8'	Bench front
10 pcs.	1x3x12'	Bench slats, cut for two pieces
14 l.f.	3/4"	Half round mold, cut
1 pckt.	3/4"	Wire brads, half round trim
2 ea.	3/8" dia.x2 1/2"	Galvanized carriage bolts
2 lbs.	#6x1 1/2"	Galvanized wood screws, bench slats

Study the plans carefully before starting construction. We suggest that you check with your utility companies to locate any underground facilities or septic lines that may be in the way.

PIERS

Mark the center of each pier at 7'-8 1/2" (center to center). Dig 12" diameter pier holes using a post hole digger to a depth 6" below your local front line. For each pier place 6" of gravel at bottom of hole, compact it, and place a brick on top of gravel.

Set 4x4 posts on top of the brick and temporarily brace post with 2x4's while making sure they are plumb and level. Make sure distance center to center of each post is 7'-8 1/2".

Fill pier holes with concrete as shown in detail "C".

Allow the concrete to cure before starting the roof framing.

ROOF FRAMING:

Build the roof framing system as shown on the roof framing detail below.

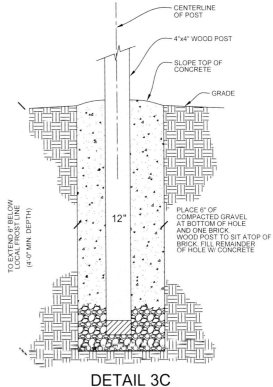

DETAIL 3C

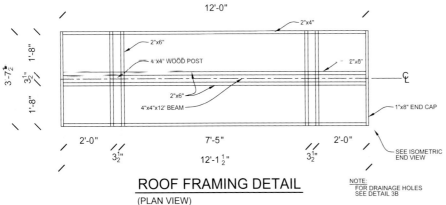

ROOF FRAMING DETAIL
(PLAN VIEW)

NOTE:
FOR DRAINAGE HOLES
SEE DETAIL 3B

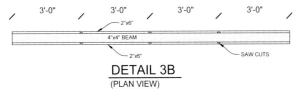

DETAIL 3B
(PLAN VIEW)

Start by making 1/8" deep saw cuts to act as drain holes in the 2x6's which are on either side of the 4x4 beam (see detail "B"). Place metal post caps on top of posts (see detail "A") and tack nail in place.

Place 4x4 beam on top of the posts according to dimensions shown on the roof framing detail above.

Pre-drill holes for bolts through the 4x4 beam.

Bolt post connectors onto 4x4 beam.

Cut four 3'-7 1/2" pieces of 2x6 to act as roof support members. Mark center line of hole for bolt and drill a hole through the 2x6. Attach 2x6 to 4x4 posts as shown on detail A.

Place the 2x6 center roof slat supports on each side of the 4x4 beam and nail to beam.

Note: It may be necessary to chisel out a portion of wood to allow for a flush fit at the bolts.

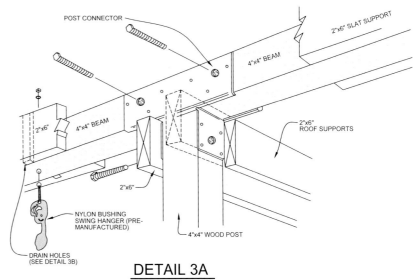

DETAIL 3A

Cut two 3'-7 1/2" long pieces of 2x8 for the end caps. Use cutting diagram shown below.

Nail end caps to 4x4 beam and the 2x6 center slat support.

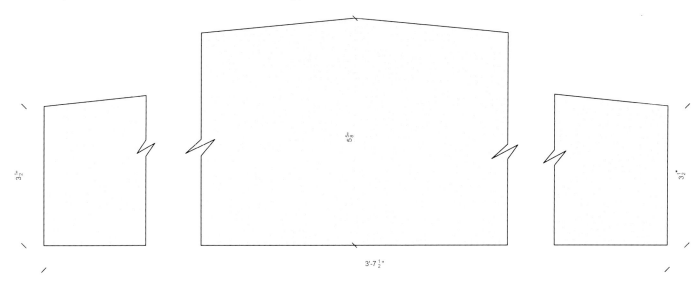

$3\frac{1}{2}$"

$5\frac{5}{8}$

$3\frac{1}{2}$"

3'-7 $\frac{1}{2}$"

Next cut two 2x4's to 12'-0" long. Nail 2x4 to outside face of the roof framing system and to the end caps as shown in the isometric to the right.

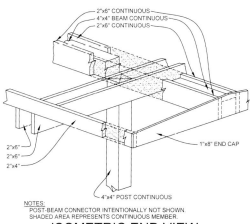

2"x6" CONTINUOUS
4"x4" BEAM CONTINUOUS
2"x6" CONTINUOUS

2"x6"
2"x6"
2"x4"

1"x8" END CAP

4"x4" POST CONTINUOUS

NOTES:
POST-BEAM CONNECTOR INTENTIONALLY NOT SHOWN.
SHADED AREA REPRESENTS CONTINUOUS MEMBER.

ISOMETRIC END VIEW

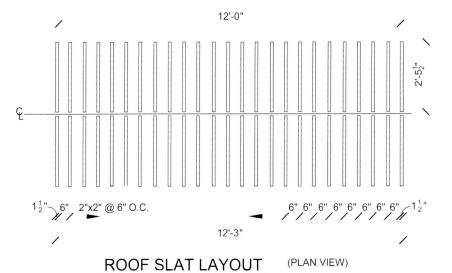

12'-0"

2'-5$\frac{1}{2}$"

C
L

1$\frac{1}{2}$" 6"   2"x2" @ 6" O.C.   6" 6" 6" 6" 6" 6" 6" 6"   1$\frac{1}{2}$"

12'-3"

ROOF SLAT LAYOUT (PLAN VIEW)

SLATS

Slats are made from 2"x2" cut to 2'-5 1/2" in length.

It is necessary to pre-drill nail holes to avoid splitting slats.

Place slats according to the roof slat layout shown above.

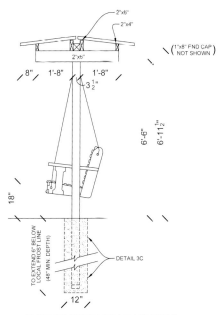

2"x6"
2"x4"

(1"x8" END CAP
NOT SHOWN)

2"x5"

8"   1'-8"   1'-8"

3$\frac{1}{2}$"

6'-6"   6'-11$\frac{1}{2}$"

18"

TO EXTEND 6" BELOW
LOCAL FROST LINE
(48" MIN DEPTH)

DETAIL 3C

12"

RIGHT SIDE ELEVATION

BENCH SWING HANGER

Place a mark at the center of the 4x4 beam for the swing hanger at 3'-1" in from the outside face of the end cap.

Drill a hole through the 4x4 beam. Install the nylon bushing swing hanger per manufacturer's instructions provided with swing hanger.

BENCH SWING

Cut out the bench framing pieces following the grid patterns shown below. Bench slats are 6'-0" long 1x3 boards.

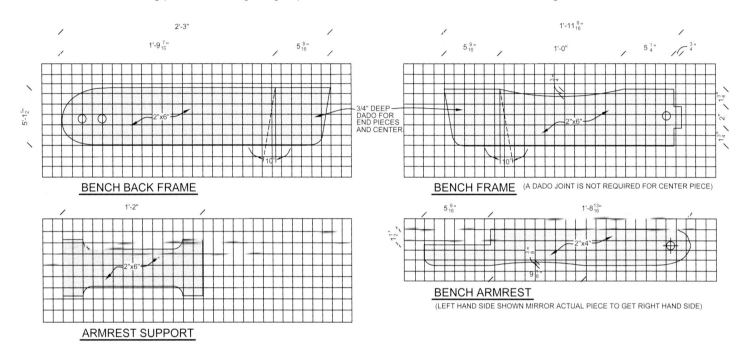

BENCH BACK FRAME

BENCH FRAME (A DADO JOINT IS NOT REQUIRED FOR CENTER PIECE)

ARMREST SUPPORT

BENCH ARMREST
(LEFT HAND SIDE SHOWN MIRROR ACTUAL PIECE TO GET RIGHT HAND SIDE)

Front face of bench is made from a 6'-0" long 1x6 board. Use bench frame dimensions shown below for the end cuts and attach all

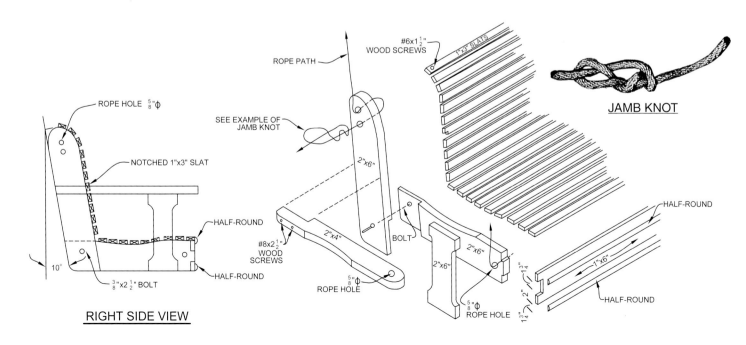

JAMB KNOT

RIGHT SIDE VIEW

pieces using screws as shown below.

ROPE BENCH SUPPORT

Make bench rope hanger using twisted fiber rope made from 4-strand extruded fibrillated polypropylene yarn (or equivalent).

Working load limits are based on approximately 10% of new rope breaking strength.

WORKING LOAD LIMITS OF ROPE:	
Diameter of rope _____	5/8"
Breaking strength _____	8,500 lbs.
Working load limit _____	775 lbs.
Color _____	Natural

Connect rope together using knots that will support the working loads shown above.

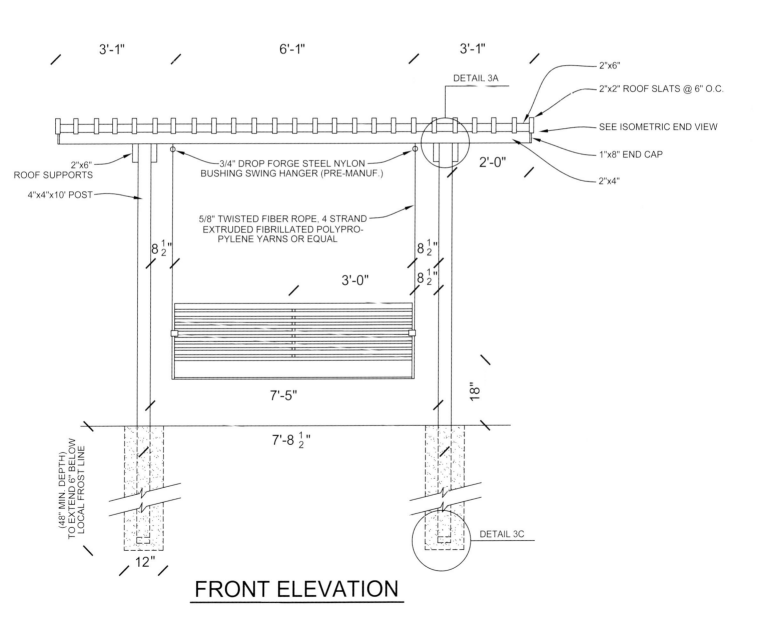

FRONT ELEVATION

The Adderly

- Size - 60" long as pictured, but length may be adjusted
- A handsome and comfortable addition to any porch or patio
- Material list included
- Step-by-step instructions included

Grammie always says to meet her at the swing after school! When we do, we can't wait to tell her all about our school day and show her the projects we worked on with our teacher that day. With her big straw hat slightly crooked on her head, she always smiles so big when we show her! Then, we climb on up on her lap and she just sways the porch swing back and forth so gently that we almost get sleepy! But, don't ever tell her we almost get sleepy, we'd never hear the end of it!

The Cajun Creek

- Size - 55" across
- Table height - 30"
- Seats eight or more on a combination of two-seat benches and single-seat stools
- Material list included
- Step-by-step instructions included

All throughout the summer months we gather around the Cajun Creek octagon-shaped picnic table on our patio and enjoy tons of laughs as the sun touches the horizon. We're so happy we built this wooden table, curved bench and single benches. Gathering here after a long day of yard work sure makes dinner taste even better, especially when surrounded by the sights and sounds of nature. We built enough seating for eight family and friends to join us on short notice, just the way we like it. We'll definitely make your next barbecue invite memorable as well as comfortable seated around our lovely table.

PLAN #F55-097D-0007

Miss Victoria's wooden English garden bench was always piled with freshly cut blooms from her wild and natural rose garden. Thorny and spindly, you sure had to pay close attention before sitting down, or you could have quite a surprise! Her timeless bench was always so inviting at the beginning of the stone path that lead to her house. I always wanted our family to have their very own garden bench like hers right at our front door. Miss Victoria kept hers natural wood, but I think I would want to paint ours to match the exterior of our humble home.

- Size - 48" x 25"
- Bench height - 37"
- Material list included
- Step-by-step instructions included

PLAN #F55-066D-0023

Adirondack style furniture takes me back to my childhood days at the Catskills under the branches of the tall oak tree just off the banks of the lake. Sometimes we'd be sipping iced tea, other times casting the reel in the perfect comfort only a good 'ol Adirondack chair provides. Not only is it a beautiful reminder of the past, but it was easy to build with the step-by-step instructions and plans. It is always the perfect accent to any patio or deck. Ours was a Traditional white, but you could easily paint yours in a vibrant color for added personality.

- Plans include all four easy-to-build Adirondack projects shown
- Material list included
- Step-by-step instructions included

The Adirondack Lake

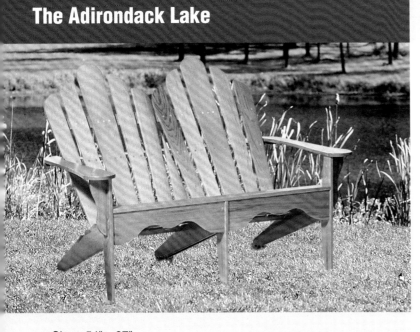

- Size - 54" x 37"
- Love seat height - 38"
- Material list included
- Step-by-step instructions included

Grandma and her cute little kitten named Socks couldn't be sweeter sitting on her attractive Adirondack love seat in her favorite shaded spot on the back patio. She often finds herself drifting off to sleep on warmer days while reading one of her favorite novels. In the evenings sometimes grandpa joins her and they watch the sunset together after dinner. The Adirondack Lake love seat really adds a cozy addition to their backyard and it looks great alongside their Adirondack chairs around their fire pit off their patio.

The Allegheny

- Size - 34" x 15"
- Table height - 19"
- Material list included
- Step-by-step instructions included

No one will forget the time when dad spilled his entire lemonade onto his lap when telling his favorite joke; you know the one where he waves his hands and arms wildly in the air! After that time, we all vowed to go looking for the perfect table that would match our Adirondack chair set. And, lo and behold, we found it! Its classic style will stand the test of time and it easily offers that extra reassurance that spills won't happen.

PLAN #F55-097D-0006

We always had so many fond memories of picnicking at our favorite park close to the house growing up. Mom would load up the minivan and bring our soccer ball, hula hoop, and other outdoor toys and we'd spend the day outdoors with family and friends. Buckets of fried chicken, Aunt Suzy's famous macaroni and cheese, and plenty of slices of ice cold watermelon would be consumed at the park picnic table on those warm, summer days. It just goes to show you that simple things can stir some of the most special memories.

- Size - 96" x 66"
- Table height - 30"
- Classic picnic style is large enough for families
- Material list included
- Step-by-step instructions included

PLAN #F55-097D-0023

The Timber Path

I was always intrigued by neighbor Carol's front yard bench. It was made from landscape timber and I could tell that someone special must have built it for her. With its somewhat compact size, it always looked so nice situated by her vegetable garden at the back of her yard. Sometimes in the summer it doubled as a spot for her big wicker basket full of veggies as she pulled them up from her garden.

- Size - 66" x 17"
- Table height - 22"
- Material list included
- Step-by-step instructions included

The Twin Cove

- Size - 60"x 25"
- Bench height - 35"
- Material list included
- Step-by-step instructions included

Sleek, simple Craftsman style always makes me think of Uncle Owen's huge workshop. He would build a twin seat bench that was the perfect design because it practically looked great with every style of home. It was so neat with its built-in place for refreshments in-between the seats. Every time we would visit I would "call" this bench on the patio at get-togethers. I can always hear Uncle Owen say, "That bench is not only attractive, but it was so easy-to-build, and no one can argue with me that it's very comfortable, too!"

The Wild Flower

- Sizes -
  Benches - 36" x 15"
  Planter boxes - 20 1/2" sq. x 17" tall
- Modular construction allows builder to configure as preferred
- Material list included
- Step-by-step instructions included

While visiting family in California one summer, we fell in love with their L-shaped bench they built for their patio. I loved how you could plant herbs, small veggies, or even your favorite variety of flowers in the three separate planter spaces, or maybe fill one with herbs, one with flowers, and one with veggies! It softened the look of the wood furniture while adding a functional place for growing your own herbs or veggies right on your patio. They said building it was a breeze, and then all they did was stain it to match their outdoor area. Oh, and did we mention it adds great extra seating space, too?

Gazebo Plans

Plan #F55-125D-3005 on page 159

A gazebo is similar to a pavilion and is often octagon-shaped. They are great additions to park areas and gardens and can be freestanding or attached to a garden wall, an existing deck or patio. They provide shade, basic shelter and architectural interest to any landscape, or garden area. Throughout American history, they have been a popular outdoor element in the backyards of the well-to-do including several of the early President's homes. Choose a gazebo plan and elevate the style in your backyard.

The Somerset Six-Sided Gazebo Plan

The Somerset six-sided gazebo plan is a sensibly sized gazebo, perfect for enhancing a garden area, or perhaps add a table and create a romantic dining space for your backyard. Its classic gazebo style suits every setting and provides a lovely outdoor focal point that will be appreciated by all.

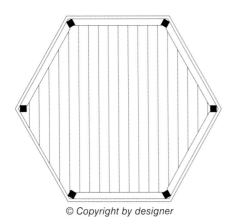

PLAN #F55-002D-3018

- Size - 8'-3" x 9'-6"
- 80 square feet
- Building height - 12'-10"
- Material list included
- Step-by-step instructions included

NOTE: All lumber is to be pressure treated.

QTY.	SIZE	DESCRIPTION
1 cubic yard		Concrete for post casing
1 pc.	4x4x14'	Wood post and 12" hex post
5 pcs.	4x4x12'	Wood post
3 pcs.	2x10x10'	Box sill, cut
2 pcs.	2x2x8'	Ledger
1 pc.	2x8x10'	Floor joists
6 pcs.	2x8x8'	Floor joists, bridging and post nailer
15 pcs.	2x6x8'	Decking
3 pcs.	2x4x10'	Decking nailer
2 pcs.	2x4x10'	Beveled top handrail
1 pc.	2x4x8'	Beveled top handrail
2 pcs.	2x4x10'	Bottom rail
1 pc.	2x4x8'	Bottom rail
3 pcs.	2x12x10'	Collar tie, cut
1 pc.	2x4x8'	Collar tie final, cut
1 pcs.	1x4x12'	Collar tie final, cut
12 pcs.	2x6x8'	Hip rafters (A), rafters (B) & headers
3 pcs.	1x10x12'	Fascia, cut
162 l.f.	1x8	"V" grooved board roof sheathing
2 sqrs.	235#	Shingles (self seal)
1 roll	15#	Roofing felt
30 l.f.		Shingle mould
26 l.f.	1x2	Lattice nailer
26 l.f.	2'-0" high	Pre-made lattice

MISCELLANEOUS HARDWARE

12 ea.		Metal rafter tie-down anchors
7 lbs.	16d	Galvanized nails
6 lbs.	8d	Galvanized nails
5 lbs.	1 1/4"	Galvanized roofing nails
2 lbs.	8d	Casing nails

This project requires good carpentry skills and knowledge of woodworking. One must have use of a table saw or be adept with a hand-held circular saw to accurately make the numerous angled cuts required to form the six sided gazebo.

After you have decided on the location for your gazebo, check for any underground utility lines that might be nearby. Accurately locate and stake underground lines.

Study the plan thoroughly.

Be sure to check your local code requirements and, if required, obtain a building permit.

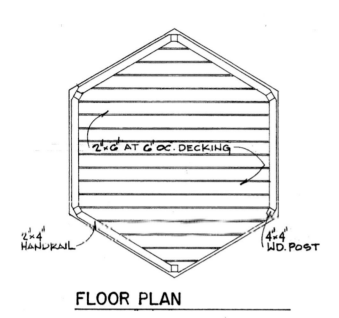

FLOOR PLAN

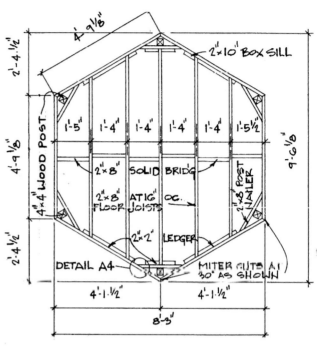

FLOOR FRAMING PLAN

Cut the six pieces of 2x10's required to form the box sill. Make a 30 degree bevel cut at each end of each board.

Nail the deck frame together using 16 penny nails. Add 2x2 ledger as shown. Cut and nail the second joist from each side in place to help stiffen the deck frame.

Use the assembled deck frame as a guide to mark the location of each of the six 4x4 posts.

Move the deck frame aside and dig a 12" diameter post hole for each post. Add 4" to 6" of gravel to the bottom of each post hole. Now move the deck frame back into position for setting the posts.

Notch the top of each post as shown in the cutting diagram, shown on the right below.

Position posts in holes with cuts to outside for collar ties.

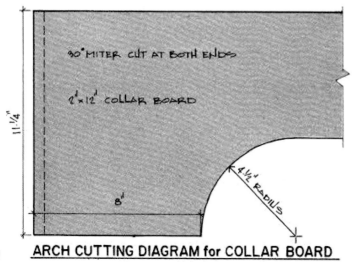

ARCH CUTTING DIAGRAM for COLLAR BOARD

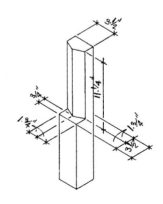

CUT POST for COLLAR BOARD

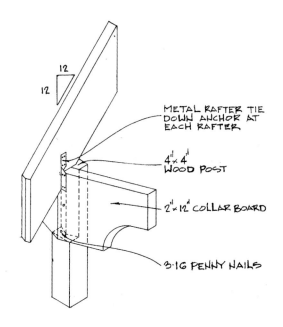

POST TO RAFTER ISOMETRIC

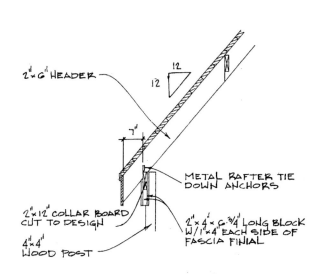

B2·SECTION AT COLLAR BOARD

Make sure that the tops of all posts are level. This can be done by placing a piece of wood across the tops of the posts and checking with a carpenter's level. If you have to raise or lower a post, add or remove gravel from the bottom of post hole.

Cut the 2x12 collar ties to size and design. Tack nail in place at the top of the post.

Plumb all posts and nail several temporary cross-ties to the back side of 4x4 to help steady the unit while you work on the roof.

Finish nailing the collar ties in place.

Start the deck frame up from the ground a minimum of 4" and nail to 4x4 post.

Add the 2x8 post nailer to the back side of the post and nail to box sill and post as shown on floor framing plan.

Add remaining floor joists and sold bridging.

Fill post holes with concrete and allow to set.

Cut and nail 2x6 decking to the floor deck framing. Allow a minimum of 1/4" between each board.

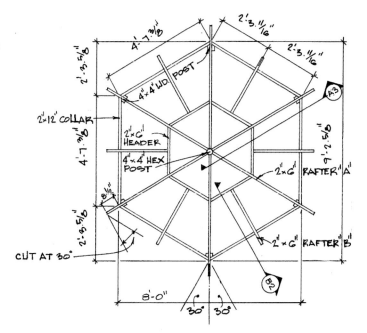

ROOF FRAMING PLAN

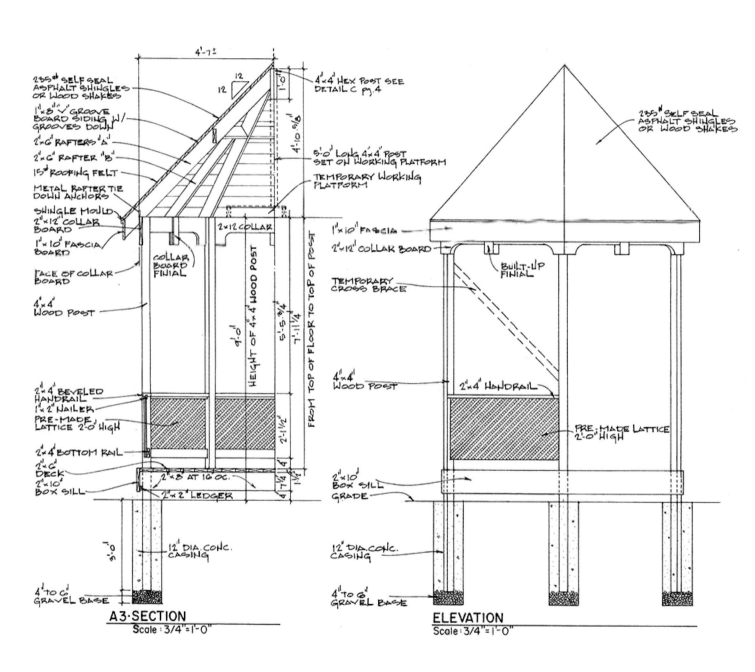

235# SELF SEAL ASPHALT SHINGLES OR WOOD SHAKES

1"×8" V GROOVE BOARD SIDING W/ GROOVES DOWN

2"×6" RAFTERS "A"

2"×6" RAFTER "B"

15# ROOFING FELT

METAL RAFTER TIE DOWN ANCHORS

SHINGLE MOULD
2"×12" COLLAR BOARD

1"×10" FASCIA BOARD

FACE OF COLLAR BOARD

4"×4" WOOD POST

2"×4" BEVELED HANDRAIL

1"×2" NAILER

PRE-MADE LATTICE 2'-0" HIGH

2"×4" BOTTOM RAIL

1"×6" DECK

2"×10" BOX SILL

4'-7 1/2"

12 / 12

4"×4" HEX POST SEE DETAIL C pg. 4

5'-0" LONG 4"×4" POST SET ON WORKING PLATFORM

TEMPORARY WORKING PLATFORM

2×12 COLLAR

COLLAR BOARD FINIAL

HEIGHT OF 4"×4" WOOD POST

9'-0"

5'-5 3/4"

7'-11 1/4"

FROM TOP OF FLOOR TO TOP OF POST

2'-1 1/2"

2"×2" LEDGER

1'-0"

4'-10 5/8"

5'-0"

12" DIA. CONC. CASING

4" TO 6" GRAVEL BASE

A3·SECTION
Scale: 3/4"=1'-0"

235# SELF SEAL ASPHALT SHINGLES OR WOOD SHAKES

1"×10" FASCIA

2"×12" COLLAR BOARD

BUILT-UP FINIAL

TEMPORARY CROSS BRACE

4"×4" WOOD POST

2"×4" HANDRAIL

PRE-MADE LATTICE 2'-0" HIGH

2"×10" BOX SILL

GRADE

12" DIA. CONC. CASING

4" TO 6" GRAVEL BASE

ELEVATION
Scale: 3/4"=1'-0"

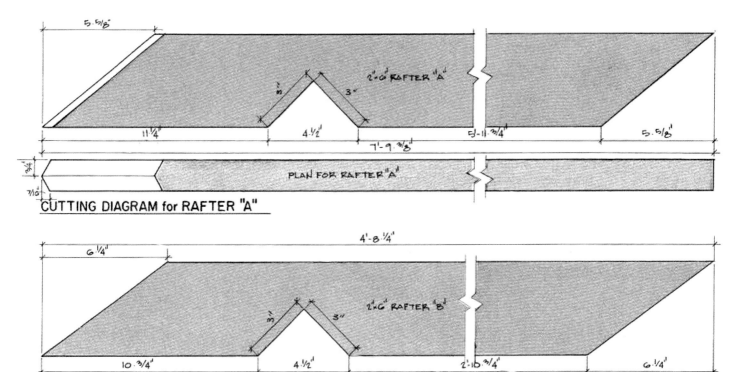

CUTTING DIAGRAM for RAFTER "A"

CUTTING DIAGRAM for RAFTER "B"

Cut the six hip rafters "A" following the cutting diagram above.

Cut the center hex post design at the top of a 5'-0" long 4x4 post (see detail C4).

We suggest that you build yourself a temporary working platform or provide some other scaffolding for working on the roof.

Brace the 4x4 hex post in place at the center of the gazebo. Set hip rafters in place and nail to the hex post.

Add metal tie-down rafter anchors to rafters and nail to collar ties.

Cut off the lower portion of 4x4 hex post.

Cut and nail 2x6 headers and 2x6 common rafters "B" in place.

Nail 1x8 tongue and groove "V" grooved board siding to the roof framing. Be sure that the finished side of siding faces down.

Cut and nail fascia board in place.

Apply shingles or wood shakes to roof following the manufacturer's instructions on product label.

Cut the 2x4 beveled top handrails to size. Add 1x2 nailer in slot on bottom side of handrail. Nail handrail in place (see section A3).

Cut and nail 2x4 bottom rail in place. Nail the 2'-0" wide lattice panels to the 2x4 bottom rail and the 1x2 nailer on the underside of the top rail.

Cut and nail fascia in place at the center line of each collar tie.

Paint or stain the gazebo as desired, following manufacturer's instructions on product label.

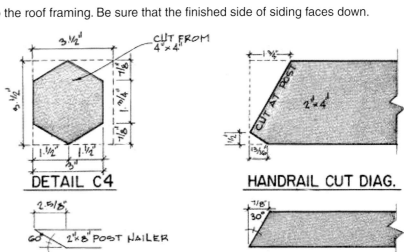

WORKING PLATFORM

DETAIL C4

DETAIL A4

HANDRAIL CUT DIAG.

END CUT DIAGRAM

The Lynn Haven

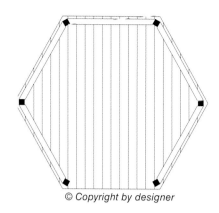

© Copyright by designer

The Lynn Haven six-sided gazebo plan is ideal for small gatherings. Its classic gazebo design will definitely enhance any outdoor area. Use it as the main focal point of your backyard, or place it in your side yard to enhance both the front and back of your home at the same time.

- Size - 10'-3" x 8'-11"
- 84 square feet
- Building height - 10'-9"
- Material list included
- Step-by-step instructions included

The Woodgrinn

© Copyright by designer

Gazebo
15⁶ x 13⁰

The Woodgrinn gazebo takes gazebo style to a whole new level with its attractive Modern square shape and its centered stone fireplace in the back. Stay warm and cozy in the great outdoors under this fantastic gazebo structure.

- Size - 16' x 14'
- 212 square feet
- Slab foundation
- Building height - 13'

PLAN #F55-002D-3000

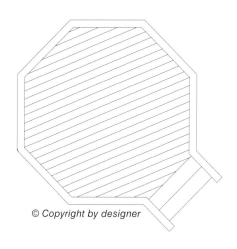

© Copyright by designer

- Size - 11'-6" x 11'-6"
- 135 square feet
- Building height - 14'-7"
- Material list included
- Step-by-step instructions included

The Windber eight-sided gazebo has plenty of space for outdoor relaxation. Add a table for alfresco dining in a garden setting, or use as a garden focal point. Either way, this stylish gazebo will not disappoint.

PLAN #F55-125D-3002

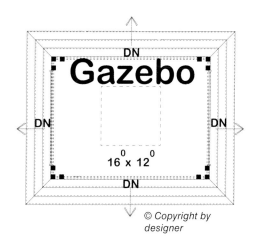

DN

DN — **Gazebo** — DN

0 0
16 x 12

DN

© Copyright by designer

- Size - 21' x 17'
- 192 square feet
- Slab foundation
- Building height - 16'

The Portland Lane gazebo has steps on all sides to make it easily accessible from all areas of your yard. The centered cupola adds additional sunlight directly below making it cheerful while still remaining cool in the shade.

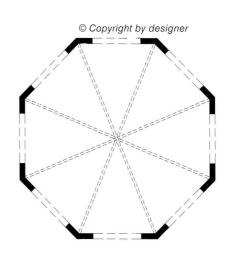

© Copyright by designer

The Bedford Lane gazebo is more enclosed than most gazebos making it an ideal choice for areas with colder weather. This gazebo has the feeling of an outdoor room with today's popularity with outdoor spaces it's sure to be a crowd favorite.

- Size - 12' x 12'
- 144 square feet
- Slab foundation
- Building height - 16'

The Sycamore Lane

PLAN #F55-125D-3000

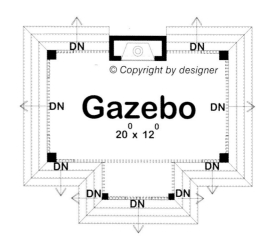

DN   DN

© Copyright by designer

DN   Gazebo   DN
20⁰ x 12⁰

DN   DN

DN   DN
DN

The Sycamore Lane gazebo has stairs on all sides to make it easily accessible from every direction. The towering stone fireplace gives it a nice cozy feel for those fall evenings when there's a chill in the air. Cuddle up around the fire and the cooler temps won't even be an issue!

- Size - 25' x 21'
- 272 square feet
- Post and pier foundation
- Building height - 17'

PLAN #F55-102D-3000

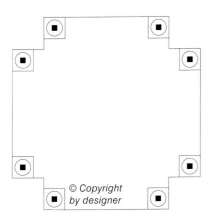

© Copyright by designer

- Size - 12' x 12'
- 144 square feet
- Material list included

PLAN #F55-125D-3003

- Size - 24' x 21'
- 365 square feet
- Post and pier foundation
- Building height - 13'

The Ossenfort Valley

The Ossenfort Valley pergola columned structure creates a wonderful shaded area for dining or entertaining outdoors. Build it pool-side for an open-air spot that's shaded for dining or cocktails, or construct it over a patio for added protection from the weather and have it extend right off of your home.

The Whitfield Hill

The Whitfield Hill is a six-sided gazebo that has beautiful style and trim work, while still being easy-to-build. Adding it to your backyard is sure to make it a special focal point that can't easily be ignored.

The Levey

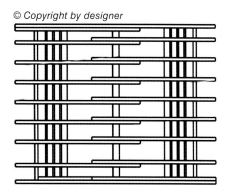

© Copyright by designer

The Levey garden entryway is a unique and attractive design that will complement your home's entry, patio or garden area. It is quite simple to build and makes a big impression in the curb appeal department.

- Size - 8' x 8'
- 64 square feet
- Building height - 10'-10"
- Material list included
- Step-by-step instructions included

The Cooper

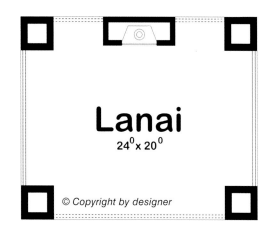

Lanai
24^0 x 20^0

© Copyright by designer

The Cooper is an amazing gazebo, or lanai that allows for perfect views when relaxing and entertaining. The fireplace in the Cooper gives it a nice cozy feel for those cool evenings. It will become the family's favorite spot when the weather is hot thanks the shade it provides, or when the temperature drops because of the fireplace.

- Size - 24' x 20'
- 480 square feet
- Slab foundation
- Building height - 18'
- Ceiling height - 12'
- 2" x 6" exterior walls

Gazebo
32^0 x 32^0

© Copyright by designer

- Size - 32' x 32'
- 823 square feet
- Slab foundation
- Building height - 21'

The Bayview Lake gazebo is a life-saver if you have an outdoor area that gets completely too much sunlight. This large gazebo is a simple style that is an easy-to-build solution that not only adds value and beauty to your home, but makes it a lot more enjoyable.

PLAN #F55-002D-3025

The Fairybell

© Copyright by designer

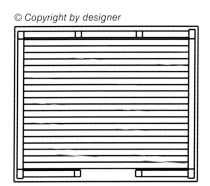

- Size - 10' x 8'
- 80 square feet
- Building height - 11'
- Material list included
- Step-by-step instructions included

The Fairybell four-sided gazebo has a gable roof and is a unique and functional addition to any backyard. Not only does it provide additional shade, but it offers added privacy when entertaining, or just relaxing outdoors.

The Maryknoll

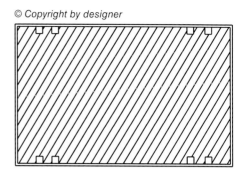

© Copyright by designer

The Maryknoll shaded deck design has a sun-screen covering that enhances your outdoor experience by shading some sunlight and making the temperature more tolerable. Near the house, or away from it, you will find yourself longing to sit underneath this shaded oasis.

- Size - 16' x 10'
- 160 square feet
- Building height - 9'-6"
- Material list included
- Step-by-step instructions included

The Sunnyvale

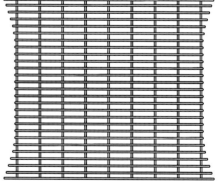

© Copyright by designer

The Sunnyvale patio cover is designed to cover an existing deck or patio, or it can be used independently as a pavilion. The design can be built with standard lumber and also includes an alternate bench design.

- Two sizes -
    12' x 13'-2 1/2"
    16' x 13'-2 1/2"
- Material list included
- Step-by-step instructions

SHED PLANS

Plan Number	Plan Name	PDF	5-Sets	Page
F55-002D-4500	The Monessen	$110	$150	58
F55-002D-4501	The Marianna	$110	$150	58
F55-002D-4502	The Carmen Cove	$110	$150	67
F55-002D-4503	The Blair	$110	$150	69
F55-002D-4504	The Blondell	$110	$150	68
F55-002D-4506	The Maddy	$110	$150	59
F55-002D-4507	The Maude	$110	$150	60
F55-002D-4508	The Marcia	$110	$150	71
F55-002D-4510	The Norbert	$110	$150	75
F55-002D-4511	The Birgitta	$110	$150	67
F55-002D-4515	The Maxine	$110	$150	59
F55-002D-4520	The Rasmussen	$110	$150	61
F55-002D-4521	The Marcella	$110	$150	61
F55-002D-4523	The Boscobel	$110	$150	48
F55-002D-4524	The Norris	$110	$150	71
F55-125D-4500	The Martha	$300	-	74
F55-125D-4501	The Marilyn	$300	-	62
F55-125D-4502	The Jennar	$300	-	64
F55-125D-4503	The Marjorie	$300	-	74
F55-125D-4504	The Abrantes	$300	-	65
F55-125D-4508	The Henwood	$300	-	60
F55-125D-4509	The Hagge	$300	-	66
F55-125D-4510	The Switchgrass	$300	-	69
F55-125D-4511	The Rosario Hill	$300	-	75
F55-127D-4512	The Terry	$60	-	72
F55-127D-4513	The George	$60	-	76
F55-127D-4514	The Domani	$60	-	63
F55-127D-4515	The Gates	$60	-	76
F55-127D-4516	The Colmar	$60	-	64
F55-142D-4501	The Penney	$875	$980	62
F55-142D-4503	The Weslan	$875	$980	66
F55-142D-4506	The Wyman	$875	$980	70
F55-142D-4507	The Fuller	$875	$980	73
F55-160D-4500	The Korbin	$310	$420	63
F55-165D-4500	The Shaw	$110	$150	70
F55-165D-4501	The Boxwood	$110	$150	73
F55-165D-4502	The Novak	$110	$150	65
F55-165D-4503	The Brinley	$110	$150	72
F55-173D-6016	The Sherry Hill	$415	$365	68

LARGER SHED PLANS

Plan Number	Plan Name	PDF	5-Sets	Page
F55-002D-7505	The McDonald	$355	$395	78
F55-002D-7506	The Oren	$355	$395	92
F55-002D-7509	The Barngat	$355	$395	94
F55-002D-7511	The Farmville	$355	$395	91
F55-002D-7515	The Pemberville	$355	$395	96
F55-002D-7521	The Barnhill	$325	$365	92
F55-002D-7522	The Barnhart	$325	$365	96

Plan Number	Plan Name	PDF	5-Sets	Page
F55-005D-7500	The Tolland Place	$250	$290	97
F55-059D-6086	The Raymar	$350	$325	91
F55-075D-7512	The Gilbert Mill	$355	$395	84
F55-095D-0060	The Lindy	$355	$395	99
F55-124D-7504	The Barclay	$635	$535	86
F55-125D-7508	The Washington Hill	$500	-	89
F55-125D-7509	The Truman Hill	$800	-	100
F55-125D-7510	The Garfield Farm	$600	-	94
F55-125D-7511	The Nixon Farm	$600	-	100
F55-133D-7500	The Chatman	$605	$495	98
F55-133D-7502	The Heath	$990	$935	93
F55-133D-7506	The Mattox	$990	$935	86
F55-133D-7508	The Harvest Run	$605	$495	90
F55-133D-7512	The Monty	$990	$935	97
F55-136D-6011	The Buckingham Ln.	$1,600	$1,100	95
F55-136D-7501	The Betz Farm	$925	$550	85
F55-142D-7513	The Eiler Creek	$1,365	$1,470	88
F55-142D-7530	The Sawmill Hill	$2,793	$2,933	87
F55-142D-7539	The Crooked Barn	$2,093	$2,233	89
F55-142D-7559	The Newfield Creek	$1,470	$1,610	90
F55-142D-7564	The Jennings Farm	$1,953	$2,093	87
F55-142D-7597	The Linfield	$2,093	$2,233	84
F55-142D-7601	The Sonoma Bay	$1,953	$2,093	95
F55-142D-7606	The Grande Pines	$1,365	$1,470	99
F55-142D-7620	The Shemlock	$2,093	$2,233	86
F55-142D-7622	The Waddell	$1,050	$1,155	85
F55-160D-7500	The Lang	$310	$420	98
F55-160D-7501	The Deltaville	$310	$420	93

CABANA PLANS

Plan Number	Plan Name	PDF	5-Sets	Page
F55-002D-4518	The Cabana Palms	$110	$150	102
F55-002D-7523	The Cesar	$575	$625	114
F55-009D-7524	The Summerville	$575	$625	116
F55-009D-7525	The Coolwater	$575	$625	117
F55-009D-7527	The Summersun	$575	$625	113
F55-009D-7529	The Sunshine Point	$575	$625	116
F55-113D-7508	The Miles Beach	$890	$1,015	122
F55-113D-7509	The Rita Beach	$890	$1,015	115
F55-125D-7502	The Raburn	$400	-	121
F55-125D-7503	The Tranquility Lane	$400	-	120
F55-125D-7504	The Bristol Beach	$300	-	119
F55-125D-7505	The Marisol Lane	$500	-	117
F55-125D-7506	The Harmon Lane	$400	-	114
F55-125D-7507	The Ivarson	$400	-	111
F55-125D-7512	The Alvarado Vista	$400	-	119
F55-125D-7513	The Maxwell Lane	$300	-	118
F55-126D-1153	The Mirage	$742	$567	110
F55-142D-7520	The Carefree	$875	$980	112
F55-142D-7593	The Carolina Coast	$1,050	$1,155	109

Plan Number	Plan Name	PDF	5-Sets	Page
F55-142D-7594	The Duck Island	$875	$980	120
F55-142D-7595	The Watershed	$875	$980	111
F55-142D-7598	The Shadewell	$875	$980	118
F55-142D-7600	The Bahama Breeze	$875	$980	115
F55-142D-7611	The Welsh	$875	$980	122
F55-142D-7612	The Rollingwood	$875	$980	121
F55-173D-7504	The Olsen	$425	$375	110
F55-173D-7510	The Allen	$425	$375	113
F55-174D-7500	The Great Cove	$450	$625	112
F55-174D-7501	The Juno	$450	$625	109

PLAYHOUSE PLANS

Plan Number	Plan Name	PDF	5-Sets	Page
F55-002D-4505	The Merill	$110	$150	124
F55-002D-4514	The Sellersville	$110	$150	132
F55-066D-3000	The Homestead Hill	$110	-	133
F55-125D-4513	The Daisy Hill	$300	-	134
F55-125D-4514	The Petunia Lane	$300	-	132
F55-127D-4503	The Shay	$60	-	134
F55-142D-4500	The Joanie	$875	$980	133

OUTDOOR PROJECT PLANS

Plan Number	Plan Name	PDF	5-Sets	Page
F55-002D-0012	The Willow Breeze	$50	$80	136
F55-066D-0018	The Cajun Creek	$50	-	142
F55-066D-0019	The Wild Flower	$40	-	146
F55-066D-0021	The Adderly	$50	-	142
F55-066D-0022	The Twin Cove	$50	-	146
F55-066D-0023	The Catskill Lake	$50	-	143
F55-097D-0004	The Allegheny	$40	-	144
F55-097D-0005	The Adirondack Lake	$50	-	144
F55-097D-0006	The Placid Park	$50	-	145
F55-097D-0007	The English Brook	$50	-	143
F55-097D-0023	The Timber Path	$40	-	145

GAZEBO PLANS

Plan Number	Plan Name	PDF	5-Sets	Page
F55-002D-3000	The Windber	$60	$90	155
F55-002D-3008	The Maryknoll	$60	$90	160
F55-002D-3014	The Sunnyvale	$60	$90	160
F55-002D-3017	The Levcy	$60	$90	158
F55-002D-3018	The Somerset	$60	$90	148
F55-002D-3025	The Fairybell	$60	$90	159
F55-002D-3026	The Lynn Haven	$60	$90	154
F55-102D-3000	The Ossenfort	$110	-	157
F55-125D-3000	The Sycamore Lane	$300	-	156
F55-125D-3001	The Woodgrinn	$300	-	154
F55-125D-3002	The Portland Lane	$300	-	155
F55-125D-3003	The Whitfield Hill	$300	-	157
F55-125D-3004	The Cooper	$400	-	158
F55-125D-3005	The Bayview Lake	$300	-	159
F55-171D-3000	The Bedford Lane	$250	-	156

What Kind of Plan Package Do You Need?

Now that you've found the plan you've been looking for, here are some suggestions on how to make your outdoor project a reality. To get started, order the type of plans that fit your particular situation.

Your choices are:

THE 1-SET PACKAGE The 1-set package is one full set of the construction drawings. A 1-set package is copyrighted, so therefore it can't be reproduced. Keep in mind, if you have to submit the plan to your local building department in order to obtain a building permit, then you would have to order additional sets.

THE 3-SET PACKAGE The 3-set package is three full sets of the construction drawings. A 3-set package is copyrighted, so therefore it can't be reproduced. Keep in mind, if you have to submit the plan to your local building department in order to obtain a building permit, then you would have to order additional sets.

THE 5-SET PACKAGE The 5-set package includes five complete sets of construction drawings. Besides one set for yourself, additional sets of blueprints will be required for your lender, your local building department, your contractor, and any other tradespeople working on your project.

THE 8-SET PACKAGE The 8-set package includes eight complete sets of construction drawings. Besides one set for yourself, additional sets of blueprints will be required for your lender, your local building department, your contractor, and any other tradespeople working on your project.

REPRODUCIBLE MASTER A Reproducible Master is one complete paper set of construction drawings that can be modified. They include a one-time build copyright release that allows you to draw changes on the plans. This allows you, your builder, or local design professional to make the necessary drawing changes without the major expense of entirely redrawing the plans. Easily make minor drawing changes by using correction fluid to remove small areas of the existing drawing, then draw in your modifications. Once the plan has been altered to fit your needs, you have the right to copy, or reproduce the modified plans as needed for building your project. Please note the right of building only one structure from these plans is licensed exclusively to the buyer. You may not use this design to build a second or multiple dwelling(s) without purchasing a multi-build license. Please call 1-800-373-2646 for more information.

PDF FILE FORMAT Our most popular plan option, the PDF file format is a complete set of construction drawings in an electronic file format. It includes a one-time build copyright release that allows you to make changes and copies of the plans. Typically you will receive a PDF file via email within 24-48 hours (Monday through Friday, 7:30am-4:30pm CST) allowing you to save money on shipping. Upon receiving, visit a local copy or print shop and print the number of plans you need to build your project, or print one and alter the plan by using correction fluid and drawing in your modifications. *Note: These are flat image files and cannot be altered electronically. PDF files are non-refundable and not returnable.*

CAD PACKAGE A CAD package is the actual computer files for a plan directly from AutoCAD, or another computer aided design program. CAD files are the best option if you have a significant amount of changes to make to the plan, or if you need to make the plan fit your local codes. If you purchase a CAD Package, it allows you, or a local design professional the ability to modify the plans electronically in a CAD program, so making changes to the plan is easier and less expensive than using a paper set of plans when modifying. A CAD package also includes a one-time build copyright release that allows you to legally make your changes, and print multiple copies of the plan. See the specific plan page for availability and pricing. *Note: CAD files are non-refundable and not returnable.*

PLEASE NOTE: Not all plan packages listed above are available for every plan featured in this book. Visit **houseplansandmore.com**, for current pricing and all plan packages available for a specific plan, or call 1-800-373-2646.

Other Plan Options

MIRROR REVERSE SETS
Sometimes a project fits a site better if it is flipped left to right. A mirror reverse set of plans is simply a mirror image of the original drawings causing the lettering and dimensions to read backwards. Therefore, when ordering a mirror reverse set of plans, you must purchase at least one set of the original plans to read from, and use the mirror reverse set for construction. Some plans offer right reading reverse for an additional fee. This means the plan has been redrawn by the designer as the mirrored version. For availability, visit houseplansandmore. com, or call 1-800-373-2646

ADDITIONAL SETS
You can order additional sets of a plan for an additional fee. A 1-set, 3-set, 5-set, 8-set, or Reproducible master must have already been purchased. *Note: Only available within 90 days after purchase of a plan package.*

MATERIAL LISTS
Many of the projects in this manual include a materials list that gives you the quantity, dimensions, and description of the building materials needed to construct the project. Some plans indicate that a materials list can be purchased for an additional fee. (see specific plan for availability and pricing). Keep in mind, due to variations in local building code requirements, exact material quantities cannot be guaranteed. *Note: Materials lists are created with the standard foundation only. Please review the materials list and the construction drawings with your material supplier to verify measurements and quantities of the materials listed.*

2" X 6" EXTERIOR WALLS
2" x 6" exterior walls can be purchased for some plans for an additional fee (see houseplansandmore.com for availability).

PLEASE NOTE: For all plan options and current pricing, visit houseplansandmore. com, or call 1-800-373-2646.

Plan pricing is subject to change without notice. Visit houseplansandmore.com for all current pricing, or call us at 1-800-373-2646.

BUILDING CODES & REQUIREMENTS

At the time the construction drawings were prepared, every effort was made to ensure that these plans and specifications met nationally recognized codes. These plans conform to most national building codes. Because building codes vary from area to area, some drawing modifications and/or the assistance of a professional designer or architect may be necessary to comply with your local codes or to accommodate specific building site conditions. We advise you to consult with your local building official for information regarding codes governing your area.

COPYRIGHT

These plans are protected under Copyright Law. Reproduction by any means is strictly prohibited. The right of building only one structure from these plans is licensed exclusively to the buyer and these plans may not be resold unless by express written authorization from home designer/architect. You may not use this design to build a second or multiple structure(s) without purchasing another blueprint or blueprints or paying additional design fees. Each violation of the Copyright Law is punishable in a fine.

LICENSE TO BUILD

When you purchase a "full set of construction drawings" from Design America, Inc., you are purchasing an exclusive one-time "License to Build," not the rights to the design. Design America, Inc. is granting you permission on behalf of the project plan designer to use the construction drawings one time for the building of your project. The construction drawings (also referred to as blueprints/plans and any derivative of that plan whether extensive or minor) are still owned and protected under copyright laws by the original designer. The blueprints/plans cannot be resold, transferred, rented, loaned or used by anyone other than the original purchaser of the "License to Build" without written consent from Design America, Inc. or the plan designer. If you are interested in building the plan more than once, please call 1-800-373-2646 and inquire about purchasing a Multi-Build License that will allow you to build the project plan more than one time. *Note: A "full set of construction drawings" consists of either CAD files, Reproducible Masters, PDF files, an 8-set package, a 5-set package, or a 3-set plan package.*

EXPRESS DELIVERY

Most orders are processed within 24 hours of receipt. Please allow 7-10 business days for regular shipping. If you need to place a rush order, please call us by 11:00 a.m. Monday through Friday, 7:30am-4:30pm CST and ask for express service (allow 1-2 business days).

EXCHANGE POLICIES

Since blueprints are printed in response to your order, we cannot honor requests for refunds.

Shipping & Handling Charges

EACH ADDITIONAL SET ADD $2.00 TO SHIPPING CHARGES

U.S. SHIPPING -	Sheds & Outdoor Projects	Larger Sheds & More
(AK and HI express only)		
Regular (allow 7-10 business days)	$20.00	$30.00
Priority (allow 3-5 business days)	$40.00	$50.00
Express* (allow 1-2 business days)	$60.00	$70.00
CANADA SHIPPING**		
Regular (allow 8-12 business days)	$37.00	$50.00
Express* (allow 3-5 business days)	$77.00	$100.00

OVERSEAS SHIPPING/INTERNATIONAL

Call, fax, or e-mail (customerservice@designamerica.com) for shipping costs.

* For express delivery please call us by 11:00 a.m. Monday-Friday CST

** Orders may be subject to custom's fees and or duties/taxes.

Note: Shipping and handling does not apply on PDF files and CAD Package orders. PDF and CAD orders will be emailed within 24-48 hours (Monday - Friday, 7:30am - 4:30pm CST) of purchase.

Order Form

Plan pricing is subject to change without notice.
Visit houseplansandmore.com for current pricing and all plan packages available, or call us at 1-800-373-2646.

Please send me the following:

Plan Number: F55-_____

BASIC PLAN PACKAGE	COST
❏ CAD File	$ _____
❏ PDF File	$ _____
❏ Reproducible Masters	$ _____
❏ 8-Set Plan Package	$ _____
❏ 5-Set Plan Package	$ _____
❏ 3-Set Plan Package	$ _____
❏ 1-Set Package (no mirror reverse)	$ _____

See the index on page 161 for current pricing for the most common plan packages. For all plan packages available and their current pricing, visit houseplansandmore.com, or call 1-800-373-2646.

IMPORTANT EXTRAS

For current pricing and all plan packages available, visit houseplansandmore.com, or call 1-800-373-2646.

❏ Additional plan sets*:

_____ sets at $_____ per set $ _____

❏ Print in mirror reverse:

_____ sets at $_____ per set $ _____

(when right reading reverse is not available)

❏ Print in right-reading reverse:

one-time additional fee of $_____ $ _____

❏ Materials list* $ _____

Shipping (see page 163) $ _____

SUBTOTAL $ _____

Sales Tax (MO residents only, add 8.2380%) $ _____

TOTAL $ _____

*Available only within 90 days after purchase of plan.

HELPFUL TIPS
- You can upgrade to a different plan package within 90 days of your original plan purchase.
- Additional sets cannot be ordered without the purchase of a 1-Set, 3-Set, 5-Set, 8-Set, or Reproducible Masters.

Name_____
(Please print or type)

Street_____
(Please do not use a P.O. Box)

City _____ State _____

Country _____ Zip _____

Daytime telephone (_____)_____

E-Mail _____
(For invoice and tracking information)

Payment ❏ Bank check/money order. No personal checks. Make checks payable to Design America, Inc.

❏ MasterCard   ❏ VISA   ❏ DISCOVER   ❏ American Express Cards

Credit card number _____

Expiration date (mm/yy) _____ CID _____

Signature _____

❏ I hereby authorize Design America, Inc. to charge this purchase to my credit card.

Please check the appropriate box:
❏ Building project for myself
❏ Building project for someone else

ORDER ONLINE

houseplansandmore.com

ORDER TOLL-FREE BY PHONE

1-800-373-2646
Fax: 314-770-2226

EXPRESS DELIVERY

Most orders are processed within 24 hours of receipt. If you need to place a rush order, please call us by 11:00 a.m. CST and ask for express service.
Business Hours: Monday - Friday (7:30am-4:30pm CST)

MAIL YOUR ORDER

Design America, Inc.
734 West Port Plaza, Suite #208
St. Louis, MO 63146

Build Your Own Shed & Outdoor Projects

SOURCE CODE **F55**

Plan #125D-4505

Plan #125D-4528

Plan #125D-4507

Plan #002D-4512

Plan #142D-7518

Plan #125D-4523

Plan #125D-7524

Plan #002D-3024

Plan #002D-4517

Plan #125D-7558

Plan #066D-0018

Plan #125D-7531

Discover a wide variety of plans that include everything from doghouses and chicken coops to studio home offices and pool side structures. Find the perfect project for you, and then build it yourself!

165

Plan #125D-4532

Plan #142D-7506

Plan #009D-7528

Plan #002D-4516

Plan #142D-7505

Plan #125D-4512

Plan #063D-4514

Plan #113D-4503

Plan #002D-7520

Plan #113D-4512

Plan #066D-0013

Plan #002D-4522

Discover a wide variety of plans that include everything from doghouses and chicken coops to studio home offices and pool side structures. Find the perfect project for you, and then build it yourself!

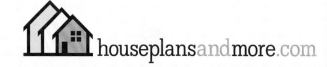

houseplansandmore.com